BARGAINING
FOR RESULTS

BARGAINING
FOR RESULTS

John Winkler

Facts On File Publications
New York, New York • Bicester, England

BARGAINING FOR RESULTS

Library of Congress Cataloging in Publication Data

Winkler, John.
    Bargaining for results.

    Includes index.
    1. Negotiation in business.   I. Title.
HD58.6.W56   1984   658.4   83-20606
ISBN 0-87196-848-7

Printed in United States of America

10 9 8 7 6 5 4 3 2 1

Contents

Preface

In the often violent and disturbed conditions which are going to prevail in the world's economies in the next twenty years, one aspect of management which is going to receive greater attention is the skill of bargaining effectively.

Managers of all kinds have to bargain their way throughout business. They do deals with key customers, they buy up companies, they land big contracts, they handle trade unions, they battle with government, they buy materials. Managers even bargain with other managers in their own companies.

When one manager who knows how to bargain faces another who does not, then the first one wins the best part of the deal. The second one gains only a fraction of what he could have gotten if he had bargained properly.

The literature, researches, practices, and customs of high level executives in seventeen countries have been studied to provide the basis for the material in this book. Perhaps two-thirds of the concepts described are unique in the sense that these ideas have not been published beforehand or described in this way.

This book is designed for a worldwide market to show the strategy, tactics and plays involved in the bargaining process. It is written with the practical manager in mind; it has case histories, practical tips, self-development questions, learning programs and game-play advice.

It will show the reader how to cope with the manipulative negotiator, how to deal with bribery, how to cause and to break deadlock, how to go to the courthouse door, how to handle pressure tactics and how to close deals.

A major influence in this book has been the experience of running over 300 seminars on management subjects all over the world. Audiences have included general managers, marketing and sales managers, finance managers, and personnel managers. Their skills and experience have contributed greatly.

Effective managers are nearly always effective bargainers. There are many books about effective management. This is one of the first about effective bargaining.

John Winkler

The Exploration of Power | 1

In February 1979, shortly after the Chinese New Year, a Singaporean businessman, Chang Soo, received in the mail a letter and a proposal from a large American company. The company was seeking an agent in Southeast Asia. Already established in Hong Kong, the company had not had a good experience in Singapore. Previously they had sought to sell directly into the market and to use a small agent in Singapore whom they could dominate. They were offering international marketing and management services.

But big business in Singapore depends, as it does everywhere else, on whom you know and how good your standing is. Their small agent could only give them access to small business contacts. He did not move in big business circles.

In deciding with whom we should do business, there is always this fundamental question to resolve. Should we go for someone small, whom we can dominate fairly easily? We can insure that he will do what we tell him.

Alternatively, should we go for one of the big companies, whose power is such that they can dominate us if we are not careful? Each market situation will be different. Two good rules of business apply and seem to run counter to each other. The first is, "Fish where the fish are," meaning that if they've got the power in the market then use them; but also, there is the other rule, "Whatever you do, dominate something." So the answer, as ever, is going to be a compromise.

Chang Soo knows about the exercise of power. He can elevate it to an art form. For him, the vigor of the Western negotiators is too crude. We lack patience, and we lack grace. The Chinese negotiator seldom says "no." What he says instead is "maybe." Chang Soo runs one of the best consultancies around the Pacific area and represents a number of international service companies.

The Pacific area manager of the American company had surveyed the possibilities in Singapore and thereby had made the first correct move in the process. He knew that Chang Soo was his best man.

Asking around the market and the trade and collecting the data and all available evidence about the other man and the alternatives for him provides one party with an enormous initial advantage. Here is the first guide towards successful bargaining:

You should start bargaining before the other man knows he's involved.

1

His second move was good too. He asked a friend, who was well respected by Chang Soo, to provide him with an introduction. The friend did so, and Chang Soo was ready to hear the proposition with an open mind.

That's the second guiding hint for successful bargainers:

> *Pre-condition the other party to have an open mind;*
> *he should respect you before he meets you.*

Probably the most valuable technique in this early stage is by word-of-mouth. If others speak well of you, you have a head start. If the other man's interest is aroused beforehand so that he comes to you initially, then you have a huge advantage from the outset. The person who makes his service scarce—the factory with very limited capacity—the dominant market leader—the company which does not need the business—they all have power at their elbow. This is because they seem to need nothing. They are strong.

Have you noticed how a salesman can always sell much, much more when he has not sufficient stock of the product? But as soon as the company builds extra spare capacity to manufacture more, then a peculiar thing happens. The salesman suddenly finds it harder. Here is a hint for successful salesmen:

> *Don't let your management*
> *expand your factory capacity.*

The area manager no doubt would have preferred Chang Soo to approach him first, but this was not possible. So, about to make the first error, the director decided to produce an outline proposal for Chang Soo to consider. Knowing correctly that the proposal itself and the way it is written, typed and presented seep into the consciousness of the other party, he made certain that it looked good. The quality of the bargainer's background is measured in such terms before the parties meet.

The proposal explained the circumstances of the company services, and outlined the benefits of the two organizations working together. It showed how the market should be tackled, what needed to be done. It outlined the role that Chang Soo's company should play, allocated tasks between the two organizations, and proposed fair and equitable financial arrangements.

Chang Soo saw before him a superb presentation. An extraordinarily thorough proposition. The logic could not be faulted. Indeed, an American company, a German outfit or a British company of any quality would have snapped it up immediately. But not an important Chinese businessman in the Far East.

That is not the way business is done there. The businessmen there are very sensitive to social relationships. They have grace, tact, and patience. They are self-effacing in their manner. Their egos are as strong as any in the Western world but it is part of their art to disguise it. The Chinese do not like open displays of strength. They want to discuss and conciliate.

Bargaining is a social exchange involving a power relationship. Before any deal is done, one party or the other sees himself as the more dominant. During the various stages, power changes from one side to the other, and back again.

Every issue negotiated is a gentle struggle for control. One team falls back while the other presses; then they pick up the initiative and move on to the attack. There is no time limit in the game. Indeed, the entire process might be over in seconds, while other—bigger—games take a long time and move through many stages.

When they finally shake hands on the deal, the power at that one moment is equal between the parties. Immediately after the deal is finalized, however, the power relationship changes again, often rather dramatically as one party relies on the other to make good his commitments.

Here is the next tip for successful bargainers:

Don't think it's over when the deal is signed.
The struggle might be just beginning.

Chang Soo decided to select one of the most valuable strategies in the armory of the successful negotiator. He appreciated the thoroughness and quality of the approach by the American company. He accepted that they were courteous and deferential. But the proposal was locked up too completely. It did not allow him to have his say. The Americans might be important in their own territory, but the Far East is where Chang Soo is important in his line of business. Chang Soo acknowledged the proposal courteously and then deployed his chosen bargaining strategy.

He did nothing. He just waited.

Power in the bargaining situation is relative. It cannot be measured in precise terms. It cannot be quantified sensibly, although factors can be weighed up and relative power can be assessed. The idea of power lies in the mind of those involved in the bargaining. One man might see his position in one set of negotiations as being very weak. There may be a lot of competition for the deal, for instance. But in another similar case his position might be much stronger. For example, he may have done business with the other party before and with a successful conclusion.

Power lies in the mind of the bargainer and it is relative to the assumed power of the other party. Here lies the next important tip for the negotiator:

The other man's mind can be altered;
but only early on.

The whole risk, the great thrill, and the immense danger of breakdown are encapsulated in this one single idea: that the expectations of the other party can be changed. But when you do it—and do it you must—you can expect to be taking a ride on an emotional roller-coaster. The trouble is that they are trying to alter your expectations at the same time. That is where the contest lies.

The American company ended up doing business with Chang Soo, and both sides were, and still are, pleased with the relationship. When Chang did nothing, the American managing director was forced to weaken his position by coming after him again. He was forced to show that he was keen to do business. Chang Soo remained non-committal for some time. The managing director asked for his views on the proposal and asked if there were alternative arrangements which would suit Chang Soo better. They agreed to a revised deal which Chang Soo proposed. It gave him better terms than are usual for the company's other associates in the world. And the American company knew it could not run Chang Soo in the way it can run the others. On the other hand, the company does better business in the Far East than it could otherwise expect, because of Chang Soo's strength in the market. As the American managing director says, "I would rather have him working for me than against me." Which leads on to another tip for the bargainer:

> *The man nearer the market place always has the edge.*
> *Ask any oilman to tell you the story of Rockefeller.*

A bargainer's power can be increased by building up his own strength, his status, the benefits he conveys with his proposition, and the reassurance he provides in the eyes of the other party. This is the route of selling, persuasion, and education.

THE BARGAINING PROCESS
Information Gathering
Diagnosis of Situation
Assessment of Bargaining Power
Setting Objectives
Developing Strategy
Structuring their Expectations
Exploration of their Needs
The Opening Moves
Obtaining Movement
Reviewing Objectives
Tactical Plays
The Settlement Area
Closure
Documenting Agreement

But he can also build up his relative power by weakening his opponent's position. He might become a little critical, he might point out the disadvantages to the other party of not doing a deal with him. This is the route of coercion and force. This requires even greater skill and care. It takes courage to walk away from the other party. It is much easier to walk towards him. And if we do use force on him, then he will use force on us in a later round of bargaining. He will be teaching us a lesson. Better not to use force unless there is no alternative.

The exchange of such pressures, the application of power, requires subtlety. Passing information about one's position to the other side, and the application of pressure, are usually carried on implicitly in the way something is said rather than in the words themselves. Crudely expressed at the wrong time, explicit pressure will be construed as an attack and will draw a counterattack or withdrawal. Certain things cannot be said out in the open, although their meaning may be clear to the parties involved. Bargaining requires a good deal of guess-work. It requires sensitivity to the position of the other party. Signalling by the use of hints is a very important part of the bargaining process. You must convey signals to them. And be ready to receive their signals to you.

Here, then, lies one further tip:

When you apply your power, do so with care,
so that they hardly notice what you are doing.

In bargaining, the strongest dictate the terms. But skill in bargaining situations, experience and knowledge, and the understanding of the other party all con-tribute to a bargainer's strength, quite apart from the kind of deal he is offering. That is what makes the interplay of this power relationship so interesting—and necessary.

SUMMARY
In any bargaining situation consider the power relationships involved. In relation to the other party will you be dealing from a position of strength or from a position of weakness? Try to find a way of building up the power of your position beforehand—for example, your power is increased if there is a good alternative for you in the event of a breakdown.

The power relationship will ebb and flow during the bargaining sessions. The tactics will include silence and stalling; and a sense of timing is very im-portant to the power relationship.

Power can be improved through research. The more thoroughly prepared and rehearsed, the more powerful the bargainer.

The Top Ten Principles of | 2
Bargaining

Before reading each chapter, you should fill in your answers to these questions in the left-hand column. Do not look up the correct answers at the end of the book when you have done so, but read the chapter first. When you have done this, come back to this questionnaire and complete it again. The changes you make show what you have learned from the chapter. Now you can look at the correct answers. Score your original answers and compare them with the second answers. That is how much *you have learned.*

Q.1   *Your job is to train sales engineers in an earth-moving equipment company. Whom should they call on first in any prospective purchaser's company?*
(a) The purchasing agent; (b) the general manager; (c) the drivers of the existing equipment; (d) whomever the receptionist suggests; (e) the shop steward.

Score   **Score**

───   ───

         Before reading chapter.   *After reading chapter.*

───   ───

Q.2   *You are disputing part of a supplier's account. He has charged you for services which were either inadequately carried out or not received at all. Do you:*
(a) hold up payment of the total account; (b) hold up payment of that part which is disputed; (c) offer to settle the disputed total on a fifty/fifty basis; (d) ask them for their "offer"?

Score   **Score**

───   ───

         Before reading chapter.   *After reading chapter.*

───   ───

Q.3   *You are the company shop steward. You do not like your full-time union area representative. Management knows this and has begun to bypass you occasionally by going directly to the area representative. You want to bring them to heel. How do you do this?*

(a) *Find an issue and pull the men out on a strike over it;* (b) *go less far than that, but threaten to do so if management does not behave;* (c) *complain to the area representative's union boss;* (d) *have some of your friends cause three or four little disputes to break out, causing production losses, without your being involved except in sorting them out.*

Score　　　　　　　　　　　　　　　　　　　　　**Score**
___　　　　　　　　　　　　　　　　　　　　　　　　___

　　　　　Before reading chapter.　　*After reading chapter.*

___　　　　　　　　　　　　　　　　　　　　　　　　___

Q.4　*When you cost a project for approval, do you prefer to:*
(a) *itemize every detail, estimate it, and cost it;* (b) *accumulate the items together, detail them, and provide grouped costings;* (c) *provide several alternatives, a kind of shopping list;* (d) *cost those items which can be specified accurately and provide lump sum figures where doubt exists;* (e) *get away without costing it at all, giving only a broad total indication?*

Score　　　　　　　　　　　　　　　　　　　　　**Score**
___　　　　　　　　　　　　　　　　　　　　　　　　___

　　　　　Before reading chapter.　　*After reading chapter.*

___　　　　　　　　　　　　　　　　　　　　　　　　___

Q.5　*You are a market research manager in an advertising agency which handles one very large account. However, your studies show that the advertising campaign is simply not working. There is a major flaw in the creative work which is putting people off. The agency is your employer. Do you:*
(a) *tell the agency and the client openly at a meeting;* (b) *let the agency executives deal with it;* (c) *analyze the figures in such a way that the result is not exposed;* (d) *simply fake the results?*

Score　　　　　　　　　　　　　　　　　　　　　**Score**
___　　　　　　　　　　　　　　　　　　　　　　　　___

　　　　　Before reading chapter.　　*After reading chapter.*

___　　　　　　　　　　　　　　　　　　　　　　　　___

Q.6　*You are the industrial relations expert. The union has asked for a 20% wage increase without any strings attached, on the grounds that that is what a comparable union has just been awarded. Inflation is running at 11%. You*

want to settle at 9% if you can, but no more than 12% at the outside because the industry is running down and in a state of decline, so profits are poor. What will your first offer be?
(a) *3%* (b) *8½%* (c) *7½%* (d) *7½% with a productivity deal.*

Score   **Score**

_____   _____

        Before reading chapter.   *After reading chapter.*

_____   _____

Q.7   *Some portable Japanese generators have fallen off the back of the proverbial truck. Normally they cost $400 each. You have paid only $50 each for them. This trade prospect wants to know how much they'll be if he takes 200 from you. His business also is of dubious legality. What do you say to him?*
(a) *Tell him of the quality and ask him to make you an offer;* (b) *to him, $100 each, but that's the first and last offer—they'll be gone tomorrow;* (c) *tell him the guy down the street is selling them for $360 each, and what would he say to $180 each if he takes the lot for cash;* (d) *$360 each, less 50% if he takes the lot for cash.*

Score   **Score**

_____   _____

        Before reading chapter.   *After reading chapter.*

_____   _____

The Top Ten Principles of Bargaining | 2

1. IF YOU DON'T HAVE TO BARGAIN, DON'T BARGAIN

Ronald Stephenson is an associate professor at the Graduate School of Business at Indiana University. With two other colleagues he made a study of over 100 companies in the American Surgical Trade Association. What he wanted to find out was whether a salesman was likely to sell more if he was given bargaining freedom to offer discounts and to vary the prices for each customer. Our logic tells us that this must be so; salesmen who have to stick to their published list prices must lose out to salesmen who are free to undercut them. (On the other hand, if the world were run according to logic, it would not exhibit the signs of incipient madness which make it so enjoyable a place to live in.)

Of the companies concerned in the study, 29% gave their salesmen absolutely no discretion on price. They had to stand on list prices, and that was that. Another matching sample included salesmen with great latitude on price. They were free to do deals with whomever they chose, their only constraint being that the more discount they gave away, the less commission they would earn.

About 40% of the total sample were given some latitude on discounts but were heavily controlled on the amounts.

The researchers thought that the salesmen with the wide authority to deviate from the list prices would sell most. They did not. They sold the same amount.

What did happen was that their companies earned least profit. Their companies' return on capital was the poorest in the industry. Their contribution to overhead and their gross profits were the poorest of all.

The salesmen with highest personal sales, but still not much above the average, were those with some latitude, but not much, on discounts.

The companies earning the highest profits and achieving very good sales per man were those who insisted that their salesmen had no leeway in the matter of price.

Other evidence shows that the price discounters create trouble for themselves. Buyers seek them out; and these are the buyers who want only to buy on price. Some people, not the majority, want low price deals. So they search for the suppliers whose sales forces have discretion in the matter. Then they squeeze them—hard.

These sales forces then return to their managements and complain that the company's prices are too high and that they would sell more if the prices were

9

lowered. They, and their management, have selected the rod for their own backs.

Here is a tip for negotiators looking forward to a long and happy lifetime ahead:

> *Don't do business with people who don't do*
> *nice business. Life is too short.*

And so to the first great principle of bargaining. Try to get into a position where you don't have to bargain. If you can get all that you want without bargaining, and if you are certain that it is all that you can get, then name your terms and hold out for them. Never betray by the merest twitch that you are willing to trade. And if you are willing to trade, make sure they realize that it is only on the minor issues, not on the central issue. Your posture, if you are selling, should be that true gentlemen do not discuss price. Your posture, if you are buying, should be that the lowest price is the only thing that matters to a businessman. Try to hold these positions for as long as you can.

Remember that you are setting up deals for the future in the way you bargain now. If you are too strong, show too much power, and you stand firm for too long, then next time they will get you. They will use force to coerce you into movement. You have taught them how to deal with you.

It is easier to say than to do. In many situations both parties expect to bargain. It may be necessary to go through the motions of bargaining and to allow the other party to win concessions which you had already planned to give away. Generally, you should only bargain if you have to.

2. BE PREPARED

Get into play before the other side. Deals are often won or lost in the first fifteen minutes of the approach even though several sessions may be involved covering many hours of debate and argument. They might not be closed in the first fifteen minutes, but that's when the structure is set up. And that, in turn, means that someone must be prepared in advance.

The bargainer who researches and prepares thoroughly—who knows where he is going and who can set up the other party's expectations—starts with enormous power. And if the other party does not know the game, or does not know he is involved in negotiations when he is in the middle of them, then the weakness of his position is extreme.

The next time you want a loan from your banker you could try nipping and squeezing instead. Asking is the nice way, the recommended way. But ask only when you know his answer will be "yes." The engineer in the following story knew beforehand that if he asked, the answer would be "no."

A large Chicago bank had a branch office downstate. One customer at the branch office was a company owned by a fairly tough engineer who had a habit of living rather well in the good years and not plowing much back into the company in the bad years. The people in Chicago had cautioned the local branch manager against providing extra overdraft facilities, although the company had been in business for some years and was sound enough.

The engineer wanted a loan for the purpose of helping to get another business started. He knew he would not get it by presenting the case, nor by any form of persuasion. He momentarily considered using a new technique, begging, but decided that it was not his style, and that the manager had probably heard it all before.

So he decided to weaken the branch manager's position. He made his accountant raise several complaints as if they were the bank's fault. The bank had been a bit slow, and the chief clerk telephoned the accountant to apologize. There was another delay by the bank in obtaining foreign currency which led to another complaint. Further complaints concerned long lines at the counter when cash was wanted, and so on. This time the manager himself apologized to the accountant. By making his accountant complain, the engineer was trying to force the bank into compliance. Then he had a stroke of fortune. The bank made a serious error in failing to credit a check to the engineer's personal account. The engineer telephoned in a towering rage. He listed all the previous bank errors and asked for a written explanation.

Two weeks later he moved in for the "Sting." The branch manager, expecting the worst, took another personal call from the engineer. He was asked what his normal charges would be for a personal loan extending over two years. Having expected another blast, he quoted the interest rates with some relief. The engineer persisted, and asked if these were likely to be the best rates on the market. "Yes," said the manager, as far as he knew, they would be. The engineer explained that he was going to make a purchase and was deciding between several different means of financing it. He took it for granted that should he come back to the bank for the money, there would be no difficulty with the loan on his personal account, given the usual guarantees. The manager agreed. Later the deal was done.

The branch manager was called on the carpet by the Chicago people for allowing the customer's total indebtedness to increase. As the manager said in his own defense, it was either agreeing to that, or facing the possibility of losing the account altogether.

He had been cornered by a customer who was well prepared, who had weakened the branch manager's position by his criticisms—the check paid into the wrong account was a final slice of luck. The engineer had been negotiating with the manager for several weeks, without the manager knowing it.

But there is another sting in the tale. The engineer made one bargaining mistake that was so disastrous that ultimately the bank manager called in the overdraft facility at a particularly bad time for the engineer. Raising the finance from other sources gave him sleepless nights. It was very expensive because some of his funding came from high interest rate sources and he was forced to give up some portion of his equity in his own company. The mistake he had made was to accept an invitation to luncheon from his bank manager at Christmas. He got a little drunk and revealed what he had done to the manager. The manager said little, but seethed with anger and determined to destroy him if possible.

Here is, therefore, one further tip for the successful bargainer:

> *Never, ever, show triumph.*
> *Let them appear to win.*

It is very important to conduct research beforehand. Find out as much as you possibly can about the other party, what are his circumstances, what are his problems. Find out who makes the decisions. Bargain only with the decision-maker; not with his juniors. But complete your research before you meet him.

3. LET HIM DO THE WORK, NOT YOU

It pays to stick to your guns if you can, particularly on major concessions. The earlier you can dig in for the battle the better, because it stops the other party from winning a mass of concessions from you later. In order for your line to be held, however, the other man's interest must be high. Otherwise he will walk away from your rigid position and you will have to weaken yourself by going after him.

When running management seminars to develop bargaining skills, an exercise is often used where one person must sell a second-hand car to another. The person with the car to sell is told that the car is falling apart and will become a liability (but he does not disclose this information to the buyer). Equally, the buyer is told that he must buy the car because it is the only model of its kind on the market (but the seller is not told this). Both parties must do the best deal they can.

It is as clear as it could possibly be that the advantages flow to the person who fights hardest over the first main issue. The buyer usually tries to hammer down the price at first and the struggle goes on for some time with the buyer refusing to commit himself to buy. Nervous that the deal might not be done, the seller is usually happy to concede new tires and the stereo unit, provided that the buyer eases up a little on his price demand. The value of these concessions adds up usually to a greater cost than the difference in price.

On the other hand, if the buyer finds himself with a seller who is intransigent on the price and who is being very difficult indeed, then if he manages to win some concession he becomes very reluctant to press very hard for other concessions, later in the negotiation. He settles, perhaps, for a fifty/fifty split on the cost of the tires and stereo.

Successful bargainers should note:

> *People derive more satisfaction from things they have*
> *worked hard to get. Give the other party this*
> *satisfaction.*

It usually pays to dig in, early on, on a big issue and stick close to the position. The effect of doing so begins to alter the other party's expectation of the final deal which might be struck.

It helps if you can get the other party to make the first bid. This now sets the limit of their expectations and leaves you free to move to the other extreme. Sometimes they will offer you more than you expect. Ask for a little more just the same; don't settle quickly because they will know they could have done better. This extra bonus you can tuck in your pocket and put down to pure technique. If you had quoted them first with your bid, then you would have gotten less.

4. APPLY YOUR POWER, GENTLY AT FIRST

Work out the relative bargaining power of yourself and of the other party and decide if you need to increase yours beforehand. Making him feel guilty increases your power, for example. Seeing him on your territory also increases your power. It is amazing how many aggravating industrial disputes occur just before the wage bargaining begins.

When a new president was appointed to a very large life insurance company, he asked his top executives if he could meet the company's more important brokers, the customers of the business. He was perfectly willing to go to them, but his executives insisted that the brokers should be brought to meet him in the company's head office and be entertained there. His executives were right in this matter without question.

Imagine yourself to be very poor. All you own in the world is a diamond mine in South Africa. It is a liability to you, you wish that someone would take it off your hands. Yet you can hardly give it away because no one wants to own diamond mines. Unbelievable as it sounds, that was the situation for diamond mine owners in that country towards the end of last century. It was not because diamonds were not popular; they were, and people paid high prices for them. The money was not to be made in producing diamonds, but in selling diamonds. The distributors had a stranglehold on the producers, a situation that was about to be altered for all time by one man.

Individual miners extracted the diamonds and sold them in competition with the production of other mines. The buyers formed a small cartel among themselves to keep the buying prices down. They forced many miners to bankruptcy.

Cecil Rhodes (of Rhodesia fame) bought out the miners and gradually obtained a near monopoly over production. Then he struck to increase his bargaining power.

He took the diamonds off the market. The buyers' ring collapsed; they offered almost any price he wanted if he would sell diamonds to them. The price of diamonds to the final customer went up many times over. Rhodes gradually released his diamonds through one company alone and by 1893 the trade was being handled on a fixed percentage basis between buyers and sellers, an agreement which has lasted to this day in a stable industry which is controlled by one of the world's most efficient monopolies, the Central Selling Organization. Most of the world's diamond production of any significance outside Ghana is sold through it.

It is only what the oil producers did to the world in October 1973—and will do again, no doubt. It is the same thing as the sudden strike by workers shortly before the annual round of wage bargaining begins. All of it is designed to demonstrate that one party can cause great damage to the other party if an acceptable deal is not concluded.

But take care: if you use pressure tactics to get your own way, then sooner or later they will do the same with you. Perhaps on the next deal.

It was Sir Harold Wilson who once said that monopoly is neither good nor bad, but it has the power to be either. We can translate this into another tip for bargainers:

> *Monopoly: it's good if you have it,*
> *and bad if they have it.*

5. MAKE THEM COMPETE

Desperation is a bad master in bargaining. The other party finds that enthusiasm and interest are reassuring; but eagerness is a sign of weakness. Instead, make them compete for your attention. If a bargainer is going to bounce the other party into a decision, then he needs a sense of timing and a rival competitor.

The owner of a printing business wanted to sell out in order to concentrate upon his other business. The business was quite small, barely profitable and was oriented toward graphic design and literature for advertising. Waiting until his lease was renewed for a favorable rent, he found himself with a negotiable asset to sell along with the business.

He set the price at a little above the value of the lease, and advertised the business for sale. He saw many time-wasters, who were not really interested. One prospect was brighter than the rest, although the prospective purchaser was rather unpleasant and demanding. Nevertheless he had a valid reason for wanting the business. The owner made the prospective purchaser put his demands in writing. This he planned to use to bounce another company into a decision.

The owner had talked with another company who also seemed interested, but it was difficult to bring them to a decision. Apparently it depended upon someone returning from California in order to run the business. The owner decided that if he were to wait any longer, it would weaken his position. He asked for a meeting with the other company and explained that he was in a fix. He particularly wanted to sell to them because it would give continuity of employment to the staff and for other reasons. He explained that he did not like the man who was making the other offer.

"What other offer?" they asked him. He showed them, in confidence of course, the letter from the other purchaser. As soon as they saw themselves losing the purchase, they came after it. The seller got his price. He would have preferred that someone else reveal the information to the other party so that he could then stand back and wait for them, but he was the only bargainer on his side, so the option was not available. Sometimes it helps to have an unofficial channel of communication to the other party.

At this moment, as you read this sentence, someone in the world is being squeezed into a deal by a competitive offer. This leads to another tip for successful bargainers:

If you panic it does not help.

6. LEAVE YOURSELF SOME ROOM

In a Texas company manufacturing pumps, the general manager could not persuade a new man to join him as sales manager even though the salary was $7,000 a year above the market rate.

The company wanted to recruit a manager for its six sales engineers. It was a good company, with considerable profit and growth potential, manufacturing well-designed products. The company had a policy of giving excellent salaries for good people—this job was advertised at $40,000 in an industry where the usual rate for this job at this time would have been $33,000. But the company did not believe in giving fringe benefits as well. The previous sales manager had paid for his own car and received a mileage allowance. There was no pension fund since the salary was large.

The general manager had the utmost difficulty in recruiting his sales manager. The best man turned it down flat, even though as it turned out his own company was about to go into liquidation, and he would be out of a job.

The problem was that the company had not allowed itself any bargaining room. The candidates came to the interview expecting this huge salary, plus a car. When they realized that they could get nothing on top of the salary, they felt disappointed and walked out.

If the company had left itself a little room to maneuver, all would have been well. If it had offered a salary "negotiable above $35,000" for example, that would have been sufficient. Or if they had made it clear in the advertisement that no fringe benefits went with the job, particularly mentioning the lack of a car, then there would have been fewer applicants for the job, but they would all have turned up knowing exactly where they stood.

In bargaining tactics, you may need to leave yourself a little room. If you want 20, then ask for 25. If you are willing to give 10, then offer 7. It is expected of you and serious damage will be done if you do not have discretion in some situations. On the other hand, you must give no indication that you are able or willing to trade. In some cases, you will not have to give anything away.

So here is the tip for bargainers:

*In the end make it just a little better
than they thought it was going to be.*

7. MAINTAIN YOUR INTEGRITY

Bargainers are not saints. Neither are they naive. Good bargainers do not reveal all their hand, tell the complete story of what they want nor why they want it. If they do so, then the other party will take advantage and will press for maximum concessions. So good bargainers reveal their information in small pieces, when it is necessary. And they never reveal the pressures they are acting under.

On the other hand, there is no need for a bargainer to be a liar. Few people question the ethics of a lawyer in the courtroom. Certainly, there may be little matters relating to his client's activities about which he would rather not know.

It is very important for the bargainer to maintain his integrity. His word must provide an anchor for the other party. If he makes a commitment it should hold. If he provides reassurance then they should be able to relax. If the other party distrusts the bargainer he becomes nervous. He may withdraw. He will certainly become much more difficult to deal with. Nervous men do not make good bargains; they demand more guarantees.

It helps considerably if the bargainer is liked personally. The signals which pass between two expert negotiators who like and trust each other are clearly understood.

A bargainer can be tough; he can have an abrasive style. He can be cunning, but preferably not obviously so. But he must be trustworthy. His word must hold. If he makes a strong demand and then climbs down, he is in a difficult position. How is he to maintain his integrity? How is his position to remain credible? He must always leave himself with a good escape route.

He must always have a good reason for moving his position. Perhaps he can be persuaded by one of the arguments of the other party. So here is a tip for bargainers:

> *If they are in a deep hole,*
> *give them a ladder.*

Through the years, Ben Thomson and Don Herbert have faced each other many times across the bargaining table. Both are accountants and when they meet, the bystanders are mystified by the conversation. They may be arguing about the argeement of some company accounts. One man makes a point, at which the other man grunts. They talk about their families. Then the other man makes a point. The first one demurs slightly, and the conversation drifts off into domestic matters again. When it is over, they do not appear to have had a conversation together, let alone come to an agreement. "We have got a good deal here," says one. The other agrees, and the observers are astonished. The two men know each other so well that they never tangle. They know exactly what they can get away with and what they cannot. The grunts are highly significant.

They came together for the first time thirty years ago when each was representing a client in a takeover bid. The negotiations were fractious and contested; the debate moved into technical areas concerning accountancy and the clients took a back seat. One of them realized that he had the other one over a barrel. There was a flaw in the presentation of the case and it was so basic that the opponent's case could be destroyed. Both men realized that the possibility existed at the same moment. Whoever it was in the dominant position at the time—and to this day neither of them will say which one of them it was—he let the other one off the hook. The other party swiftly made covering noises and asked for an adjournment. They signalled to each other in technical language where the settlement area existed without their clients knowing what was going on. They made their recommendations and the deal was done. The clients were a little mystified that it was wrapped up so quickly, but both parties were satisfied with the outcome.

8. LISTEN, DON'T TALK

Unless the other party interacts with you, you cannot move them. The person who asks the questions generally is exerting control over the relationship. He is forcing the other party to give him feedback, by disclosing information about his position. Armed with this information, he can then modify the shape of what he wants to say, in order to suit the needs of the other, or to work on the other party's pressure points.

The bargainer must reveal his own information and his position to the other party as well. Inevitably he must present his case, and debate the issues. But it helps enormously if the other party has revealed his own situation first.

The bargainer who times his presentation correctly, only reveals enough of his own position to arouse the interest of the other party, asks the necessary questions, and listens carefully to the answers is in a strong position. He will pick up problems well in advance, he will spot opportunities, and he will be able to judge accurately the limits of the other party's position. Then, when he does talk, he will do so in a way which suits the other party. He will minimize resistance.

The chairman of any committee should be neutral; but he has a supreme advantage over his colleagues. He can make them all talk first, he can ask questions, and then he can sum up. He will sense what is possible for this committee to accept; he can influence them to adjourn, or to put back any decision he does not like. He can sum up the points he does like, and weaken the opposition's argument by ignoring others. He can do all of this without revealing where he himself stands on any particular issue. That is how chairmen retain control while remaining officially neutral.

There is a guide for successful bargainers in this:

> *Be less of a lawyer,*
> *more of a judge.*

9. KEEP CONTACT WITH THEIR HOPES

It pays to make high demands and then stick to them. It pays also to have an excuse available if you do have to climb down. (*See* principles 1 and 7.)

But there is a limit on the amount you can demand. If it is set too high, then you will achieve deadlock. The other party will withdraw, and will brush your demands aside. If you are in a conflict bargaining situation, where the gains of one party represent the losses of the other, then the deadlock resulting from this will cause you strikes, if you are in industrial relations; legal actions if you are in contract together; and the recall of ambassadors, or trade sanctions or war, if you are in international politics.

Very high demands need to be floated, signalled first in order to set up the expectations of the other party.

Each spring, in a certain Connecticut town, a boat fair is held, resulting in a very substantial sale of second-hand items of boating equipment. Private individuals sell equipment, as do members of the trade in order to clear out their old inventory for cash. Many visitors do not attempt to get the prices down any further because they feel reluctant to bargain when prices are already at rock bottom. But much haggling does go on, and both parties—buyers and sellers—seem to enjoy it.

Life jackets usually cost about $50 new. One dealer was selling them for $38 new on his stall. A passer-by rather aggressively told the dealer that he would offer him $28 for one. The dealer refused to talk to him about it. Shortly afterwards, the dealer overheard one man saying to his wife that he wanted to buy a life jacket and he thought he had passed a stall earlier where they were being sold new for $25. He asked her if she could remember where the stall was. They both began to walk off, when the man appeared to notice the life jacket on the dealer's stall. He said, very gently, that he supposed the dealer was not willing to let it go for $25, was he? He said that his wife and children were near to starvation because he had this 40-foot boat to pay for, etc., etc. They both laughed, the dealer grumbled a bit about the customer taking the shirt off his back, but sold him the life jacket for $25.

It may be a very small incident to relate in a book about bargaining, but the technique was displayed fully in the fifteen seconds or so during which the transaction took place. The first buyer lost because he lost contact with the dealer on price. His abrupt offer of $28 was too far below what the dealer wanted. The dealer did not like him, and would not deal.

But in the second case, the conversation between the husband and wife was premeditated. Deliberately but not obviously, and within earshot of the dealer the man signalled what he expected to pay. They moved off, causing the dealer to think he was losing a prospective customer. Then, with gentle badinage, they closed the deal.

Hint for bargainers:

> Don't believe everything you overhear.

Make high demands, but keep contact with their hopes. The further the distance between what you want and what they want, then the more you have to signal, the more you have to make them come after you until you are both within sight of each other's expectations. Then, and only then, can you make your bid in the open.

Otherwise you will lose them.

10. LET THEM GET USED TO YOUR BIG IDEAS

Go for the top. Go for the most you can get. And don't come off this top limit of your aspirations too easily.

The previous example of the man buying the life jacket cheaply was also a good illustration of the use of signals in bargaining technique.

Signals are of immense help in negotiating technique. They show when the other party's demand is too strong. They indicate the high level of your own aspirations. They set up the other party to expect a certain kind of result. They provide an indication of when movement is possible and in which direction solutions can be found. They will cue-in the other party to prepare for a trade-off; to link concessions; to expect rejection or to locate the final settlement area.

If you deliberately want to drive them towards deadlock, as part of your strategy to alter their expectations, then do not use signals. Make your demands clear and unambiguous and prepare for the shock-horror reaction. Later, when you want to indicate where your extreme demands might possibly be modified (in return for a concession on their part, of course) then you can use signals again. They will get you in the same way the next time of course. If there is a next time.

It can pay you to carry a parachute into the bargaining room, as any public relations consultant knows. When the client asks him how much he will charge, he opens it out in the upper atmosphere and gradually floats it to earth until they see it in their sights. That is his price.

When companies ask public relations consultants to provide a quotation for their services, then the company concerned is always in a quandary. Their services can always be built up to a figure which the client is willing to afford. But they know that if they force a client to name his budget then there will be a tendency for the client to quote a relatively small figure. This is not to the liking of the public relations consultant, who would rather have a big client than a small client.

So, many of them use a signalling process whereby they show the prospective client the kind of work they do for other clients—all of whom are large. When the prospect asks how much the budget of the other client is, then the public relations executive watches his reactions closely. If he does not exhibit shock-horror at the answer, then the public relations executive knows that the figure quoted does not frighten the prospect. But if the prospect demurs quickly, then another example of the consultant's work is shown, this time costing less.

If the consultant is still not certain, then he can either provide a basic proposal plus extra projects each costed separately; or he can provide a kind of shopping list of projects. The more attractive ones for the client, those with the greatest likely benefits, are nearly always the projects which lie in the higher cost bracket. Here is a recommendation for physical exercise for the bargainer:

Practice your shock-horror reaction in the mirror
each day, when you brush your teeth.

The use of third-party case histories is extremely valuable to a negotiator. By quoting them he can signal almost any intention to the other party, without actually making any commitment, and he can learn to judge the likely reaction of the other party to his moves before he makes them.

SUMMARY

If you are very strong and the other party needs you then name your deal and hold out for it. If you do this, then do so with great courtesy—your action will seem boorish and arrogant, so you must increase the amount of personal warmth you offer, otherwise they will withdraw or seek revenge on the next deal. Always be well prepared; better prepared than the other party. Try to get them to make the moves if you can. Indicate, but gently, that they have a little competition for your services; this will weaken them and make them more eager to work with you. Provide yourself with a little leeway, just in case you may need to make a concession or two. Be trustworthy, reliable, and deliver more than they expect. Listen hard to what they say and the way they say it, and do not be too greedy. Why not? Because if you are too greedy they will walk out on you, or if they cannot do this then they will get their own back later. Give them some time to come around to your way of thinking. Better if they come to the conclusions for themselves, rather than your making up their minds for them.

*   *   *

Now go back to the quiz at the start of the chapter and complete it again.

Laying the Foundations for Results | 3

Here are some questions about you and your bargaining experiences at work. You must answer truthfully, and you must answer quickly. Circle the appropriate letter. Answers at the end of the book.

		Very true of me	Usually true of me	No feelings either way	Usually untrue of me	Very untrue of me
1.	I enjoy bargaining experiences	A	B	C	D	E
2.	My mind sometimes wanders off during boring sessions	A	B	C	D	E
3.	I enjoy analyzing what has happened in negotiations	A	B	C	D	E
4.	When I come to think of it, what I do at work is really rather unimportant	A	B	C	D	E
5.	I generally leave preparation until the last minute	A	B	C	D	E
6.	If a negotiation failed I would be depressed	A	B	C	D	E
7.	I would be happier in a job where I made things	A	B	C	D	E
8.	I find buying and selling things dull	A	B	C	D	E
9.	I dislike having my deals evaluated by my superior	A	B	C	D	E
10.	There is another kind of job I would prefer to do	A	B	C	D	E
11.	I work hard, most of the time	A	B	C	D	E
12.	I worry about not doing well, sometimes	A	B	C	D	E
13.	I am more interested in my home life than in my work life	A	B	C	D	E
14.	I try my hardest to get it right, all of the time	A	B	C	D	E

Laying the Foundations for Results | 3

The program controller on duty at the BBC Television Studios in the West of London at 5.00 p.m. on Monday, May 5, was hardly moved by the dull set of programs due for transmission that evening. So how could he possibly have been prepared for the fact that within 30 minutes he would have negotiated and completed deals with American, European, African, and Middle Eastern television networks, deals which were worth hundreds of thousands of dollars and upon which the overseas networks required an instant decision and instantaneous transmission from BBC TV? Moreover, the demand was so strong that they were prepared to pay almost any price and would not take "no" for an answer. Only the networks in the Far East did not demand satellite transmission. Their audiences were asleep in their beds, so they were willing to take only the transmission at normal "news" rates for the next day.

In bargaining, there are many, many occasions when you cannot be prepared in advance, and when you must rely upon experience and skill alone to do the best deals. Such deals are opportunist; they are of the "take it or leave it" kind; the offer is usually too good for one party to turn down. Where such deals are done, it would seem that it is pointless to attempt to prepare in advance. But this simply is not so: enormous gains can be made by a negotiator who is trained to handle any surprising contingency. Only a minority of airline pilots have experienced an air disaster—but how many lives have been saved through regular practice in handling such emergencies in simulator aircraft?

Remember that the other party might have been preparing his position for some time. He may have been bargaining without you knowing it—and now he is going to bounce you into an instant decision. You must be prepared for these emergencies. This is the classic way of the company takeover which is resisted. Men have made fortunes on such tactics.

The BBC TV controller found himself with an emergency bargaining situation on his hands. The price was not even mentioned because such emergencies have occurred in the past and a standard price has been established; the BBC could not squeeze the last drop of revenue out of each customer simply because there was not enough time to do so, and on the next occasion it might find itself on the buying side, instead of selling. It could then be squeezed harder.

Six days beforehand, a group of five dissident gunmen had taken hostages in the Iranian Embassy and were demanding the release of some prisoners from jail.

The police had carefully prepared the ground for their negotiations with the terrorists over the week. They knew who their protagonists were, in which rooms the hostages were being kept, all about the terrorists' backgrounds, finances, arms and training. Gradually, the police moved into a position of control by means of cutting all the other communications links except their own. They used delay to establish gradually a relationship with the terrorists and to lower their expectations.

The gunmen's original objective was to have many dissidents released from Iranian jails. Gradually the police moved them away from this extreme position to a point where they were instead demanding publicity for their cause. This was granted, but the tricky stage was then to make it clear that they could not be given an airplane in which to make their escape, and that they all would have to be arrested and stand trial. This was now the sticking point for the gunmen.

Delay is one of the most valuable weapons in the bargainer's armory. If someone wants something badly, but his demands are too strong, then the other party should simply go quiet and unresponsive, and should take his time.

The other valuable weapon is to use only one communication source through which all messages must be passed. Companies without number—particularly large multinational companies—destroy the efforts of their own managers, by channelling communications to their suppliers and their customers through too many different levels and involving too many different people. The legs are cut off their salesmen time and again; and the hands are cut off their buyers. Their efforts are undermined by someone else in the company—and often this other executive lies higher up at a senior level.

There is a tip for bargainers here:

*You should talk to many of their people; but all
their people should have to talk only with you.*

But the situation at the Iranian Embassy had altered in mid-afternoon on the Monday. The terrorists realized that they were failing and decided to raise the stakes. They shot a hostage, and told the police they would shoot another every half hour if their demands were not met.

Now the police were to act; they warned the news reporters that something was about to happen. So the news cameras were trained upon the scene and the world's television programs were broken into to provide instant "live" coverage. The police deliberately wanted the operation publicized around the world so that it would be clear to all would-be terrorists that in England they run a high risk of being killed. (They all were killed, except one youngster.) The police were setting their reputation for the long term.

Within an hour the siege was over. Men of the anti-terrorist SAS squad were lowered down the outside walls. They threw stunning bombs into the rooms; they shot the gunmen, and threw the hostages—literally threw them—to safety. The world watched a slick and efficient military operation.

At the time of the attack, the police were deliberately talking on the telephone to the leader of the terrorists, ostensibly making arrangements to meet his demands. Thus they were using deception for the first time; they were providing signals which indicated the reverse of what they actually intended doing. It points up another principle, touched on in the previous chapter. If you are going to cause deadlock in order to alter the situation dramatically in your favor, don't give them an indication of your intention. Hit them with the full extreme demand in one move. Then let them get used to the new situation. But be prepared for their counter move.

The point is that every move the police made, every move by the military, was planned in detail and rehearsed. Several alternative moves were also practiced but not used. Success was gained in Princes Gate, London; but its foundations were laid in a military academy located in the West Country.

In laying the foundations for successful bargaining, the stages are: preparation, analysis, rehearsal, and review.

Preparation
Bargaining is about the technique of applying power; and knowledge is power. Knowledge is born out of two factors: one is information and the other is experience. There is no substitute for the dull gathering of facts and information, and turning these facts into a plan.

Analysis
Analyze the other party's situation; look for the benefits of your propostion which would appeal to him. Try to assess his pressure points—what will he lose if he does not do the deal with you? Analyze your own bargaining power and increase it relative to his, if possible. Then determine the level of your first offer and your overall strategy.

Rehearsal
In the late seventies in New York, one management training company grew at a phenomenally fast rate. Few of their competitors realized how quickly the business had expanded. Part of their success lay in the fact that every morning, executives, managers and assistants met for half an hour to practice their selling skills in role-playing situations. Is it to be wondered at that they were so far ahead of competition when it came to selling their services?

Foreigners doing business in Germany are frequently surprised by the thoroughness of the German preparation. Almost every question seems to be anticipated. It is commonplace for German management to rehearse important deals; even the smaller companies do it. It gives them their strength and reputation as effective bargainers. But it is also their weakness. They can be caught out by the completely unexpected proposition.

"Role play" the negotiations in advance; not once or twice, but five times. Use different people to play the other party—some nice, some nasty. Let someone play Devil's Advocate and think up every possible objection he can raise.

Tip for bargainers:

It's nice to have the status of a gentleman.
But the card sharp always wins.

Review

During the negotiating sessions and after it is all over, you must review the progress and the tactics. You must always keep in mind the original objective— the other party may have been successful in whittling away some of your expectations. Keep the whole deal in sight; spot the lessons of success and of failure.

If you are not your own worst critic, then you may be dangerously complacent. How can you improve your skills if you are satisfied with your performance? If you are reading this book for yourself, that is a good sign—if you are reading it to see if it should be read by your subordinates, then sit back quietly and think about yourself.

David Lane is an investment banker at a well-known Wall Street firm. His life is spent in putting together deals and introducing people who might be useful to one another. After every deal, whether successful or not, he makes a note of his own performance on a series of record cards. He notes the causes of success and the causes of failure; he is sternly self-critical.

He has found that his behavior has moved in cycles. From his records he can find periods when he tended to talk too much, other periods when he became lazy in preparation, other times when he was not taking enough risks in his own approach and relying too heavily on his experience. He finds that it is possible for an old mistake to recur, such as not asking the right kind of questions. He is constantly monitoring his own performance.

Question for bargainers:

In nature, matter either grows or it decays.
Are you growing your bargaining skills deliberately,
or allowing them to decay?

THE FACTUAL FRAMEWORK

A vast amount of effort goes into the training and briefing of company negotiators and salesmen about the company's own products and performance. For the majority of companies their representatives go to the market armed only with this information. And that is a very bad practice.

Product and company information is vital, but much more information is needed than this. Having product knowledge is less than half of the requirement.

APPLICATION KNOWLEDGE

The first requirement for the negotiator is to understand how the features of his proposition will be of benefit to the other party. These benefits need to be quantified. It is almost useless to state that "our service engineer lives only 25 miles away from you."

Better to say, "Would it interest you to know that our service can save you an average of $30,000 a year?" This is then backed with a chart showing the cost of breakdown to the customer, and the money likely to be saved through having the sales engineer located close at hand.

Such data as this cannot be thought out on the spot. It needs to be planned into the presentation beforehand. A buyer will evaluate and quantify proposals from several suppliers if he can, even if he has already decided with which company to deal. He squeezes the chosen supplier with this information which is presented in a way which is favorable to the buyer's arguments. The pieces of information which do not suit the buyer's arguments are carefully left out. Buyers use far more tactics and plays upon salesmen than salesmen use upon buyers. They have more scope for game-play because they generally exert greater power.

It is vital to know how the other party will make use of your proposition; how it will be applied; what problems it will cause; what the alternatives are; and what the ultimate benefits are to the other party of accepting your deal.

OPPONENT PROFILE

The most valuable data to have is that which relates to the other party. We must be certain of the decision-making process in the other party's organization. We must know whether the person we deal with can deliver his side. Negotiating with the wrong person is probably the most common error made by newcomers to the game. The top bargainers always go close to the center of authority in the other party's organization. No one else can say "yes" or "no"; no one else has their level of discretion.

Tip for bargainers:

> Be careful of middle managers.
> They often have the power to say "no"
> without having the authority to say "yes."
> You must get to the "yes" man.

A supplier's negotiator must establish the personal position, power, and authority of the buyer. He must know how decisions are arrived at in the other organization. Who decides that a new piece of equipment is necessary; who searches for alternative quotes; who screens them; who does the technical evaluation; who can veto the decision; how is it to be financed; how is the final decision to be taken, and by whom? He should keep a record card with this information and this record should contain details of previous transactions.

Equally the buyer's negotiator needs to know the scope and authority of the seller's negotiator. If he wishes to have the terms and conditions varied, can this executive agree or must he refer any decision higher in the organization? How badly does the man himself need the business? How important is the business generally to the other company?

It is helpful if bargainers know the first rule of buying:

BUYING/SELLING: OPPONENT PROFILE

Personal Characteris-tics:

Age
Family Status
Background
Career
Hobbies and interests
Personality
Attitudes to: negotiator
                 products
                 organization
                 competitors

Organization Characteris-tics:

Type of company
Employees
Financial size
Product line
Markets served
Their competitors
Current situation
Organization structure
Pricing policies
Promotion policies
Distribution methods
Development plans
Need for our specific business
Problems currently faced

Buying Procedures:

Searching procedures
Decision-making procedures
Product analysis
Value analysis
Vendor analysis
Individuals involved
Timing quesitons

Selling Procedures:

Selling strategy
Marketing strategy
Selling organizaiton
Pricing methods
Discounting methods
Negotiable terms
Key individuals
Selling pressures

*Find out if the other party has any
discretion and then get it from him.*

If the other party is too difficult to deal with, then you must get behind him or above him. He must receive pressures upon him from his own organization acting in your favor. But such pressures must be exerted before the bargaining begins; once it starts, the other party collectively begins to close ranks. So research the information beforehand—and research it thoroughly.

COMPETITIVE PROFILE

Probably the weakest area of all in terms of factual data relates to competitive information. This answers the question: "If the other party does not do a deal with me, then whom else will he go to—what are his options?"

In conflict bargaining situations, such as in trade union disputes or contract disputes, there is no sensible alternative for the other party. This means that a deal must be done in the end between the two parties. In these situations, usually the gains made by one side represent the losses of the other. Nevertheless, it is usually the strategy of the weaker party to such negotiations to search for an alternative market for his proposition, or to attempt to set up a collaborative bargaining situation.

"Look, if our guys go on strike for any length of time, then you'll have lost them altogether. They'll get other jobs."

(Union leader)

"We are not going to get anywhere like this. We can always sub-contract the work they do. But if you agree to alter the working practices so we can produce more, then we will have a little more in the kitty for everyone."

(Company personnel officer)

This is a straightforward example of both parties putting on a little competitive pressure for their services, and one party trying to produce a collaborative deal.

If you are buying, there should always be competition around the corner waiting to supply you. It may be implicit in the conversation, but it exists there, in the atmosphere.

If you are selling, then the product should always be in strong demand. The company's policy should always be to look after favorite customers but let the others look after themselves.

Neither buyer nor seller can possibly know about all competitors' offerings all the time. What is important therefore is for the negotiators to know about their *closest rivals*, and to know about the *market leaders*. Sellers should always have detailed knowledge of at least one competitor who is above him on selling price—and he should have detailed knowledge of one competitor who is below him on quality. Buyers should have similar information available about alternative suppliers.

COMPETITIVE PROFILE
Major Competitors/Suppliers
Major Product Groups
Major Applications
Strength/Weakness Analysis in:
Product Performance
Service Performance
Price/Discount Performance
Promotional Performance
Market Performance
Credit Performance

Both parties should make an analysis of the strengths and weaknesses of their respective competitors. Much of the negotiation may turn on a discussion of the merits and demerits of doing business with these. This is where pressure points will lie; this is also where opportunities lie.

THE BARGAINING TEAM

Theoretically, the ideal size of a bargaining team is one—you. That way you have total control over your own side. Control is the biggest difficulty in team negotiations.

However it asks too much of one man to observe his other party, to be fully expert in every aspect of the discussions, and to be agile enough to develop flexible alternatives instantly. Also it cuts out team tactics, which might be useful.

There may be experts introduced on the other side. You must cover them; so you move to the next ideal size of a bargaining team—yourself and one other, with you in charge.

You may find yourself faced with a large team on their side. Be careful, the decision-maker may not be present; they may be there to press you for information and that is all.

When faced by a large team, don't make yours larger. Make yours smaller, but just as expert. In that way, your team members gain in authority.

Your aim is to divide and rule the other team. Look out for supportive action indicated by any member of the other team and re-inforce him. "Can Peter tell us what he thinks now?" you might say, having noted that Peter agrees with you and disagrees with his own team. The other team will have problems of self-expression, they will contest with each other to demonstrate their individual seniority and status. This is to your advantage. You might, with your small team, even get yourself into the position of a neutral chairman, actually adjudicating between their views.

Big negotiating teams are not popular in this book. But if you have to have one, then sort out who is going to be team leader, through whom all the communications must flow. Your members must not talk directly to their members in public, only through you. Your members must be individually briefed as to their role and objective, and rehearsed. The most senior executive in the team must be subordinated to the requirements of the team leader. And the team leader is the only one who is allowed to offer concessions. He must have communications control.

Really top men save themselves for the finish. Commodity brokers in Cairo will expect to see keen and eager young men who first sort out the basics of the deal before their boss is flown out later, to be wined and dined in the plushest of surroundings and then to make the final little concessions to wrap up the package.

The young men's task is to explore the situation and report back on the likelihood of success; the two sides set up the bargaining area, and it is this aspect, the analysis of prospects and the setting up, which is so important. The final closure involving the bosses is usually a ritual. A good tip for bosses is, don't give your team any leeway, unless you like throwing money away. And if you want to do the best deal possible, then do it yourself.

Every five years or so, the owners of gasoline stations in Europe play a ritual and enjoyable game called "Stripping the Seven Sisters," referring to the seven biggest oil companies in the world.

Every five years or so, the contracts for gasoline stations come up for renewal. The negotiations are often difficult, because oil companies want to cut back on their weak sites and want to develop strong sites. It is common to find four or five oil majors surveying a good site, offering financial help to develop the site, making recommendations as to the property itself as well as offering business development plans and finance. The gas station owners are shrewd and often hard dealers, with extensive interests in car sales. So they know what they are doing.

Most oil companies lift the negotiations out of the hands of their normal area representative. The real estate manager, the financial adviser, the area and regional managers all go to see the customer. He winds them all up one by one, extracting the maximum concession from each and offering the threat of giving the site to a competitive company.

In one outstandingly successful oil company, they ensure that their area representative handles the full deal from beginning to end. Rarely does the area manager become involved. If he does, then he acts as chairman to the discussion, not interfering. He places his seat midway between the customer and his own executive, watching both. If deadlock is to be caused, then he causes it by telling the customer that the demands are too high. He never concedes anything significant—that is always done by his executive. The manager plays the hard man; later the executive may say quietly to the consumer that he thinks he can arrange for a little extra concession. Team tactics are played.

In this way, the local executives become very strong in their own areas. They are seen to be the decision-makers by their customers. It is no use trying to go over their heads. They bring in their own managers to prove to the customer that they have reached the end of their terms. Their own managers are a help to them by standing firm.

In most companies managers take the legs out from under their own men by giving extra concessions, often just to display their own status.

Tip for bargainers here:

Any boy can give it away;
it takes a man to say "no."

THE BARGAINING PLAN

The bargaining plan is a key document and lays the basic foundation for the negotiation. It should be codified, measured, and written down for every member of the team to understand.

It is very important that the plan sets a limit upon the amount of freedom which will be allowed to the bargainer. If the bargainer is allowed to "secure the best deal he can," then he will be driven down to his bottom limit. If he is shored up by a previous instruction or by an advance commitment to a goal, then he will be more effective and will complete higher value deals.

However senior the bargaining team leader, it is always important for him to have a boss back home to whom he reports. If he wants to take a hard line then he can do so by blaming his "boss," without the issue becoming a personal tussle of will.

It may pay dividends if the team leader does not know the bottom line. In the United States, special squads of police negotiators are trained to handle hostage situations. They talk with the abductor, gain his confidence, make friends with him and gradually bring him around to the idea of giving in. If the Chief of Police decides that the issue can be resolved only by shooting the abductor, they will not tell their own negotiator this. They have learned their lesson from one incident when the negotiator knew that the police needed the abductor to come outside to his car when they were going to shoot him. When the man said he was coming out, the negotiator warned him to stay inside! If you set out to make friends with a man, then remember that he makes friends with you, too.

There is a tip for bargainers here. Remember that you have to bargain inside your own company with your own boss:

Get your boss to agree to give you a blank check.
But never give one yourself to subordinates.

There are six stages involved in the planning process. These are: diagnosis; prognosis; setting objectives; drawing up the strategy; tactical maneuvers; and control.

The factual summary of the present situation should be written down and the evidence assessed. What is our present situation, what do we need? What is their present situation, what do they need? This basic two-part question needs to be broken up into the many aspects of a complex deal. The information should be quantified as far as possible. There should be a search for the collaborative possibilities and the opportunities for linking issues should be identified. The *diagnosis* of the situation should take into account the factor of time. How will time affect the situation? Will delay work to our advantage or to theirs?

The second stage, *prognosis*, is a judgment of what will happen in the case of the parties not getting together at all; or in the case of deadlock being reached. What will be the position of each party in turn? This shows the amount of bargaining power which can be applied on each side. It will also disclose whether this power needs to be built up further in advance. The power relationship will be determined more by the penalties of not doing business together, rather than the benefits of doing business. This prognosis stage will also help to determine how the approach should be made—a very important matter in the art of successful bargaining.

Then, the specific *objectives* need to be agreed and written down. These will include the long-term objective which may stretch beyond this particular set of discussions; it will include an overall objective for the deal; and it will include a series of minor objectives for individual parts of the deal. Also these objectives will each contain maximum and minimum limits. This represents the bargaining room with each objective.

The next stage is to determine the overall *strategy* for each section of the negotiations. Will the negotiations involve: persuasion? coercion? manipulation? the use of third parties? collaboration or conflict? quick thrust or prolonged pressure?

The detailed *tactical* moves need to be planned. Who must do what? When and how should things be done? The budget needs to be agreed, and so does the timetable.

The final stage is very important. Each phase of the negotiations needs to be *assessed* against the original expectations. Is the other party responding as anticipated? Have they made unexpected demands? Have they conceded more quickly or slowly than we expected? Have they dragged us off course in any way? Are we getting enough, could we get more? Do we have to revise our estimates of possibilities? These are the essential things to review. It is never any use having a nice well-thought-out plan if the actual performance is not measured against it.

Bargainers should take note:

> *The results are always wrong when compared*
> *with the plan. But they are better than*
> *if there were no plan.*

SUMMARY

The foundation for success is to have a plan, based upon sound information. First of all assess what it is you have to offer, and calculate how they will use it. Know your own case very well; but equally find out about the other party. Find out also about the competition, how much does the other party rely upon your proposition alone? If he has alternatives available to him, what are the strengths and weaknesses of your case versus his alternatives?

Then assess how the deal will be done; who should be involved on your side at each stage of the process? What role should each person play? Keep the communications flow tight through your own team leader; if you use an expert on your side he will be an asset to you when facing laymen, but this will be neutralized if they introduce their own expert.

Above all, have a plan worked out. Set objectives, work out how they are to be reached, and review the situation constantly.

Bargaining Behavior | 4

Before reading the next chapter, fill in the answers to these questions in the boxes. Then read the answers and complete your scores. These questions need only be done once.

Q.1 *On your 44th birthday you have been left $100,000 by an aunt. You want to invest this money for the long term, after you retire. You need professional advice; and you know seven people you could ask. Whom would you approach?*

(a) A stockbroker; (b) an agent who sells mutual funds for a life insurance company; (c) an insurance broker; (d) a banker; (e) a personal financial advisor; (f) a lawyer handling trust investments; (g) an accountant; (h) all of them.

Score

Q.2 *There are several possibilities they could recommend to you. Given no other information than their jobs, which would you expect to be their principal recommendations for you?*
    Circle only one investment for each. Each type of investment may be recommended by more than one adviser.

		Adviser						
		a	b	c	d	e	f	g
1.	Investment in equities bought in the stock market	·	·	·	·	·	·	·
2.	A savings & loan account	·	·	·	·	·	·	·
3.	A new and larger house to live in	·	·	·	·	·	·	·
4.	A good pension fund	·	·	·	·	·	·	·
5.	Life insurance, linked to mutual funds	·	·	·	·	·	·	·
6.	An insurance endowment policy with profits	·	·	·	·	·	·	·
7.	Gilt-edged investments, municipal bonds	·	·	·	·	·	·	·
8.	Investment in a private company	·	·	·	·	·	·	·

Score

Bargaining Behavior | 4

Scrutinizing the small print on an office lease is not most people's idea of fun. But if the scrutineer is in a towering rage at the time, as was the one in the following story, then for a moment that lease becomes the only important thing in the world.

The owner of this rather pleasant nineteenth century building was supposed to be responsible for the repairs and decorations to the hall ways, according to the lease. The occupiers had taken a lease under an oral promise that the stairs and hallways would be decorated shortly. They needed access quickly, so they signed.

Poor deals nearly always occur when you are pressed
for time.

One year later, and after several letters to the managing agent acting for the owner, the painting on the stairways and halls remained one year older and one year dirtier. The occupiers found it embarrassing to invite customers to their offices.

The managing agent for the property was stalling on the issue, saying that the top floor still was not rented, and if the decorations were to be completed, they would be damaged again later when new tenants moved in. But the managing agent was deceiving the occupier on the issue, because the top floor had been taken off the market.

It was the discovery of this deception which caused the occupier's temper. He searched the lease to find a legal hold on the owner but it was worded in too vague a fashion for the satisfaction of a court. To refuse to pay the rent would lose them the lease if they were taken to court. In any case, going to court is a certain way of playing a Lose–Lose bargaining game and is to be discouraged. Unless, of course, you yourself are a practicing attorney in which case you can look forward to playing a Win–Win game with the attorney acting for the other party. There is nothing a lawyer likes more than a rich client who wants to stand on his rights.

There is a message in this for bargainers:

Examine the courtroom door as often as you like,
but never go inside.

Going to court provided no answer for the occupier, so other tactics had to be deployed.

The bargaining process is a social exchange; as in all social transactions, the way in which the parties conduct themselves is at least as important to the outcome as the bargaining strategy involved. Provided that a negotiator can get his proposition into a position where it can be compared to the best offers available to the other party, then the one who wins will be the one who is regarded as the nicest/best/most reliable/most reputable/most efficient negotiator with whom to work.

All these factors are intangible. They have been carefully built into the minds of the other party. The way in which a negotiator conducts himself is taken as the strongest indication of the quality of the organization he represents. His social style is important.

The tenant judged himself to be dealing with an inert opposite number who was taking no notice of his demands. He must be brought to heel and made to respect the tenant. Pleading was out—they had tried that without success.

The first question to be answered was—who was the owner of the property, what was he like, what were his pressure points? What was the character and nature of the managing agent?

From an examination of real estate records, the tenant discovered that the property was owned by a family company which itself was controlled by a senior partner in the actual firm of managing agents for the property. This partner had now retired from day-to-day participation in the business, but the firm still carried his name. So the managing agents and the owner were now seen to be one and the same.

The senior partner was still a man of some standing in the community. He was on several company boards, including that of a local savings & loan. The tenant sensed that the owner might be susceptible to an appeal for personal help. His sense of honor and his reputation would help; certainly he would not want to be caught up in a messy controversy. He would not be actuated by profit considerations.

The managing agent was assessed as being a strong and determined personality who knew, by past experience, that he achieved his best results by taking a strong line with the tenants in his properties.

The first tactical requirement was to "wrong-foot" the managing agent, and to separate him from his superior, the owner of the building. A polite and carefully worded letter was sent to him reviewing the history of his broken promises. It was written for the record so that it could be produced as evidence later in the bargaining process. This letter gave the managing agent four weeks to start the repainting, without specifying any threat. A reply was not expected, and neither was it received. This was later to embarrass the managing agent with his superior.

On the day the four-week deadline was up, another personal letter was sent by the tenant couched in the most courteous terms, and asking for personal help in the matter. It enclosed a copy of the previous letter to the managing agent, and was sent this time to the home of the senior partner.

It offered apologies for encroaching upon the retired man's time, "realizing that you no longer have a controlling influence over your subordinates," etc. and suggesting that it was a pity that ethical standards had slipped so much since the time that he himself was running the business. This touched the senior partner exactly on his pressure points; but it did not offer any threat in any way, nor did it impose a deadline. But the owner had been brought up in a hard school and was made of sterner stuff. He used stalling tactics, and delayed his reply.

Now events moved toward their climax. The tenant took a set of black and white photographs of the worst parts of the decorations. These were made to look bad. With an apologetic note, these were sent to the senior partner at his home, with a letter—"We know you probably have not seen the property for yourself and do not realize how bad it is," etc.

Sets of these photographs were also sent to the homes of each member of the board of the owner's company—mostly these were relatives of his. The intention was for them to put pressure on him and for him to find a way out by blaming his managing agent.

The photographs were not sent to the managing agent. He would be left out of control and in a position of weakness. It was intended that he would experience the utmost difficulty with his superiors.

Here is a lesson for bargainers:

> *If they are standing still, then get them moving.*
> *If they are moving, then get them running.*

Within two weeks the decorators were in the office building painting and repairing the halls and stairways.

If that had not been done, then a further escalation of the pressure would have been exerted, this time directly upon the managing agent. He was a member of the executive committee of the local Real Estate Association covering the area. The next stage would have been for the tenant to tell the managing agent that he planned to send a set of photographs to each member of the committee (his professional competitors), and to the national body, together with a history of the dispute and asking for their advice.

The managing agent never had a chance really. He was bound to collapse in the end.

There is a lesson for bargainers in this:

> *To get movement from the other party*
> *use the nice way first, not the nasty way.*
> *But remember you have a choice.*

Conditioning the other party

The process of bargaining requires that we alter the behavior of the other party; we condition him to move in a way that suits us. In this chapter we shall look at the process of such conditioning; the social interaction that takes place; the creation of effective communications flows; and the problems of identifying and countering manipulation when it is used upon us.

To cause any behavioral change we must first alter the attitudes of the other party. We must therefore start with their preconceptions, their existing beliefs, their needs and wants and move them towards our proposition.

The other party will go through a series of reactions which are very similar to the learning process. We must first assess them and their drives—collectively as an organization, and separately as individuals. Then we provide them with a stimulus, usually in the form of a proposition which appeals to them. This stage of the process is known as "respondent conditioning."

The presentation of the benefits in our propostion to them acts as a stimulus. But their interest will also be aroused by our presentation of a problem or difficulty which they perceive but cannot themselves solve satisfactorily.

This will attract a response from them. The exchanges from this point onwards involve a process of shaping their responses towards our point of view, while they in turn will be shaping our responses towards their view.

This shaping is undertaken by means of either positive reinforcement providing them with encouragement and social reward when they say something favorable to our case, or occasional negative reinforcement by offering resistance or withdrawal when they do not support our case. This is known as "operant conditioning" because the consequences occur after the other party's behavior which has caused them.

The tenants of the building saw that they must move the managing agent away from his rigid position. The owner of the building originally was not involved and would not even know what was going on. So heavy negative reinforcement was used on both parties. The pressure was intense and determined. There was a series of unrelenting moves.

Later, after the dispute had been settled, the tenants were to offer an olive branch. This would show the managing agent that it would be better to co-operate with the tenants rather than fight them. The tenants were subsequently helpful in supporting an application of the managing agents to the local court for permission to change the use of the top apartment from domestic occupation to offices. This was a difficult application, but the managing agent got it through with the help of the tenants.

This is what is meant by shaping and conditioning the behavior of the other party. Such conditioning extends well beyond the time scale of the immediate set of negotiations. It determines the longer-term pattern of the relationship. Such reinforcement, either positive or negative, leads to modified behavior and is the purpose of the bargaining exchanges. This "teaching" process is not one-way—while we are acting upon them, they are also acting upon us. Such vicarious learning is obtained from watching the behavior of the other party. This affects the future behavior of each towards the other.

In bargaining practice, the debate is usually conducted along fairly logical lines. But the interaction between the parties involved is on a more personal and mildly emotional level. In the end the issue might be resolved upon the degree of sympathy existing between the parties. But afterwards, negotiators always rationalize the result and provide a logical analysis. Few people ever say: "We did not do business because he did not like me enough."

Some self-justification may be needed to shore up a wounded ego if a negotiation is unsuccessful. "We don't want to do business with his kind anyway," or "The man's a fool," are common reactions to failure.

If you want to move the other man your way, then you will have to understand him and sense what he wants. Stimulate him to pay attention to what you say and to react to you. When he agrees with you, then support him; when he disagrees with you, then provide either no support or gentle resistance.

And if you want him to go along with you, then you will also have to go along with him sometimes.

When a bargainer is faced by a wide range of alternative choices, then the evidence is that he pays a great deal of attention to rational factors. A precise, measured and quantified case is needed to get into his mind at this stage. He is similarly impressed by such a case at the beginning of the bargaining process.

But later on, when he has narrowed down his choices, then the evidence shows that his personal aims and feelings begin to predominate. These include his friendship with the other party, and the emotional bond which has been established between them. These factors become important towards the closing stages when the decision is tight. To win a deal without establishing any goodwill between the parties is possible but only when no options are sensibly available to the weaker party. But most marginal deals will be nudged into success by the party that has established the stronger rapport.

BARGAINING MOTIVATION

Bargainers have two broad sets of pressure acting upon them. They must respond to their own personal drives, and they must act also in their professional role on behalf of the organization they represent.

When the company negotiator deals, he tends to steer a careful course between satisfying his own personal needs and those of his organization. He has his own aims and ambitions and he tries to do a satisfactory job for his organization at the same time. So he can be swayed by personal pressures as well as organizational pressures. The "mix" of the two is not a fixed ratio for all people— some are less influenced by personal motives than others. Neither is it a fixed ratio for the same person for all time.

The company negotiator is affected also by the decision-making group behind him. Behind the scenes will be his superiors, peers and subordinates—many of them with a direct professional interest in the outcome of the deal. There will be people who will evaluate the offerings; people who can veto the decision; people who want to influence it; others who want to approve it. He must complete a deal which can be carried through all of these people, most of whom he may never meet.

In order to shape the responses of the other party it may be necessary to go behind him, and exert pressure from a third party. "A" might be weaker than "B" but want to do a deal with him. If "A" is stronger than "C" and it is known that "C" has a hold on "B," then "A"'s result can be obtained by going through "C" and making him do the work.

For example, a small team has made $150,000 in five years through recognizing this principle. The only cost to their company has been one telephone call.

It is a business employing commercial artists. They are too small to be officially "recognized" as an advertising agency, which means that if they place advertising on behalf of their clients then they are not allowed any agency commission— usually 15% is payable by the newspapers and other media to officially recognized agencies.

A client of theirs wanted to advertise on commercial radio and they were asked to compose a commercial to go with their advertising designs. The client asked them to book the time. They faced two options—they could try and get the commission through the back door from the radio station, perhaps by offering to pay in advance. This, they knew from experience, would not work; or they could try and link up with a fully "recognized" agency who would be willing to split the commission with them. In the strictest sense, this is against the rules of the advertising world but the practice is widespread. The trouble with this approach was that any agency of any size would want to split the commission on at least a fifty/fifty basis, if not with the balance in the agency's own favor.

They calculated that the local sales director at the radio station wanted their business. That made them strong in relation to him. They also calculated that the sales director would have a number of friends in the advertising agency world who would do him a favor by taking on a split commission deal for him. He had done many favors for agencies in the past, so there was certain to be one who would owe him a return favor.

There was. A deal was agreed that the cash would be paid promptly for the radio time and in return the agency would take the normal credit from the radio station, do no work except to book the time, and cut back 12½% to the artists, keeping 2½% for itself.

The artists placed all their press advertising, radio, and some television through the agency on this basis; this totalled about $1,200,000 over five years, netting the artists $150,000.

This kind of story reinforces the point that preparation and research are vital. We cannot suddenly switch the strategy halfway through a discussion. Therefore the question which is always the primary one is: what moves these people, what do they want, what can we make them want; if we cannot influence them ourselves, then who can?

If you want to influence the other party then you should be popular. Most international oilmen would rather deal with the Saudi Arabian negotiators than with the Libyan negotiators. The Saudis are polite and hospitable; they are quite demanding in what they want, but they always offer a hand of friendship.

But the Libyans will keep oilmen waiting for months before even seeing them. The oil executives' proposals are likely to be torn up and thrown on the floor. They are likely to be personally insulted and degraded. No top oil executive in his right mind would ever go himself to Libya; he will send his junior men. Moreover, he will give them very limited terms of reference so that they can make few concessions.

The Saudis are universally popular in the oil world. There are few companies existing who would not be more than willing to do them a favor any time they asked. It is not absolutely necessary to be popular to be a negotiator; but miserable personalities are seldom "stars" at the business.

Sometimes you will want to obtain your results by being a hard man, to use your power to press down the other party. It is always better to be able to call upon a bank of personal goodwill, so that when you must hold out for what you want you can do so without disrupting the relationships. Friends can stand the occasional strain in a relationship. But enemies use it as a basis for revenge.

To be popular requires a man to indulge in socially rewarding behavior. Dominance can be sought, but it must be combined with sufficient warmth of manner. For instance, no man can become chairman of a public company without having teeth that can bite. But usually, the top company chairmen are personally hospitable, charming, gracious, and sociable.

The skilled social performer will adapt his own role to that which is expected of him. His social stance is quite flexible. He will be very attentive to cues and signals coming from the other party. With experience, he becomes highly sensitive to some cues. An experienced negotiator will always be able to pick out key words, phrases, and actions by the other party which indicate significant movements in their position. Such signals may go unobserved by outsiders, but they take on special meanings in repeated negotiating situations.

His assessments of the other party are made extremely quickly, and where doubt exists he will seek confirmation by asking questions and by a visual examination. Never forget how important it is to observe the other party. Their voice, their manner, their posture, their expression will all reveal the intensity and direction of their meaning.

Social rewards can be based upon the other party's needs for dominance, dependency, recognition or self-esteem. Social punishment can consist of frowning, looking away, looking bored, disagreeing and so on. Social control is exerted by rewarding the other party for the desired behavior, and punishing them for other behavior.

All social behavior involves elements of deception. The self which is presented is partly bogus. We look more confident than we might feel, perhaps, and the more discreditable features of our personality are disguised. Because of this, it is extremely dangerous to deliberately attack the other party's self-esteem, unless it is a calculated part of the negotiating strategy. It is so dangerous that we can say, almost, it should never be done. It will bring a response which will often be violent and unpredictable, and it will inevitably bring a counterattack. Reason and logic will give way to high emotion.

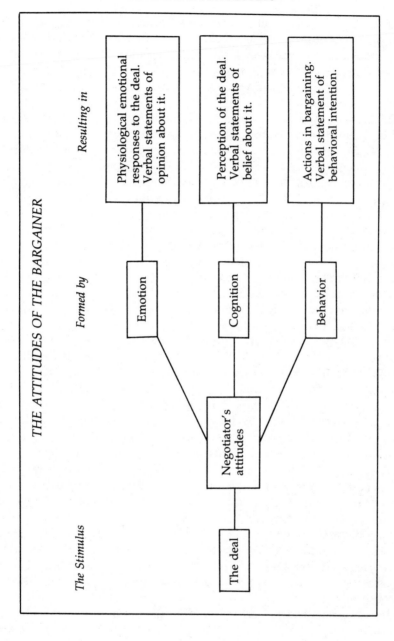

THE ATTITUDES OF THE BARGAINER

The Stimulus   Formed by   Resulting in

The deal

Negotiator's attitudes

Emotion — Physiological emotional responses to the deal. Verbal statements of opinion about it.

Cognition — Perception of the deal. Verbal statements of belief about it.

Behavior — Actions in bargaining. Verbal statement of behavioral intention.

If you are going to attack the other man's plan, or his company, or his colleagues—so be it. But always make it clear that you except him, personally, from the criticism. Naturally, you realize that he himself is equally as embarrassed as anyone, and the fault is not his personally.

Look out for the signals of their emotional state. The way they stand may tell you whether they are relaxed or tense; how near or far they position themselves from other people (including you) will provide you with clues about their degree of friendliness. Their gestures will tell you of their inner state and will often reveal or confirm their attitudes. Their eye movements will reveal whether they are interacting fully with you, or are planning withdrawal. Their speech patterns, if lucid, denote confidence and preparation; but if they are interrupted, this denotes a state of emotion and uncertainty. Their facial expressions and their orientation may reveal more than a thousand words about what they are really thinking.

Bargainers should not feel left out of this:

You provide signals to them as well.

There is one further behavioral problem that should be mentioned and that is the problem of perception. It is a fact that people have a tendency to see only what they wish to see, and to hear only that which they wish to hear.

Two individuals will each give a slightly different interpretation of a set of circumstances. We are discriminating in what we choose to remember. Everyone involved in a bargaining situation is trying to find a sense of balance between three elements. These are: their *beliefs*, what they think is true; their *emotions*, what they feel is true; and their *actions*, what they see is true.

To cure problems of perception it will be necessary for you as a negotiator to take some stages very slowly. These are the facts which are very important for the other party to understand. Often such facts relate to the limitations of what you are proposing. Now this is very difficult for any negotiator who is uncertain that the other party will make a deal. The proposition must be made and its weaknesses outlined after the other party's interest has been aroused and confirmed.

Take the issue slowly, and cause the other party to feed back to you what they understand by the proposal in their own words. It is no use saying: "Do you understand that?" because their answering "yes" is meaningless. The question must be "What effect might that have on you?" or, simply, "Would you give me your reaction to what I have just said?"

There is a temptation to fudge the tricky issues which you know they will not like; the more the negotiator has "bent" his argument to suit the other party, the greater the tendency to gloss over the issue when it comes up again. Equally, they may be fudging an issue for you; they may actually want you to misunderstand them, because they know you would object if you knew the truth. The seeds of later disaster and conflict are sown in this way. The best advice is: spell it out for them; don't overdo it, but make certain they understand the limits of your proposition. It will serve you well in the long run, although you may lose a little in the short term because of your honesty. In this way you can live with yourself, too. And this shows through in your manner.

Advice for bargainers about tricky issues:

> *Be bold. March towards the sound of the guns*
> *—provided your army is bigger than theirs.*

THE MANIPULATIVE BARGAINER

Spotting the manipulative bargainer takes skill and care. He does not become noticeable for some time during the discussion, but after a while, you may begin to sense that something is wrong.

Initially the manipulative negotiator will behave as any other skilled bargainer. He will probably have a *pleasant manner* at first; this is in order to keep you at the bargaining table. But you will find that he *prolongs his objections*—as soon as you settle one point he will move to another, and he might even move back to his original point later. He does this in order to press you for your maximum concessions and to lower your expectations.

He will give little information away, and his *reactions will be controlled.* He will *defer his decision*, and become noncommittal. If he makes demands on you, *he will "sell"* these to you with good reasons attached as to why you should concede them.

But so far, he has done only what a sound negotiator will do. He will, if he can, get the proposer to agree to his demands, one by one, without any commitment to the deal on his part, and he will start with the most important concession and work down the list.

To counter this, the proposer should ask for the complete list of the other party's requirements on the basis that only when the whole picture is known can a reasoned judgment be made.

But the truly manipulative negotiator will use either a strategy based on domination, or a strategy based upon subservience.

One of the two dominance techniques is based upon the characteristics of a "born leader." This man is so overwhelming in his power that his authority is difficult to resist. He will make you feel inferior if he can, and you will be pressed into doing what he wants. To counter this move, the opposite technique of withdrawal is required.

The other dominance technique is displayed by the fierce critic. A series of complaints and criticisms may be used and are usually associated with simulated anger in order to force the other party into a compliant role. To counter this, if placating him does not work, then the other technique is to play an end game, described in a moment. We are dealing here with artificially induced emotions; if the anger is genuine and the emotion expressed is true, then no manipulative intent is involved and the negotiator can respond as he normally would to an emotion of this kind.

Of the two subservience techniques, the most familiar is one of flattery, encouragement, apparent help and apparent support proffered for the negotiator. This may be thoroughly manipulative in intent; its purpose may be to cause you to do a great deal of work, or to reveal all your information while there is no intention of doing a deal with you. This is often the tactic used by buyers who want to see salesmen put forward proposals in order that they can use them to squeeze their chosen suppliers. All professional buyers do it from time to time. The counter to the technique is to spot it early and then to withdraw. They may be shocked, hurt, etc. but if they are genuine then they will come after you. If not, they won't.

Watch out for the sham negotiator, as in this case.

A company chairman felt there was something wrong with one of his divisions. He asked the division president to talk with a consultant about the problem. The division president was apparently very pleased to do so. He set up all his colleagues to meet the consultant; he wined him and dined him. He was apparently eager himself for the consultant to start work, but his colleagues were resistant. It had been put to them gently that this fellow would come in and tell them how to re-organize their operations.

He flattered the consultant by his attentions. But the consultant found that none of his own suggested approaches drew any positive response. Neither the division president nor his team gave the consultant anything at all to go on.

The consultant gave up in the end. He collected a survey fee, and told the chairman that it was not an assignment to suit him. He had been manipulated, and skillfully, by the managing director. That, actually, is most of what was wrong with the company in the first place.

Tip for bargainers:

Even if you are the company chairman, it
does not mean that you always get your own way.
You are in the hands of your subordinates.

The final manipulative strategy is withdrawal. In a locked-in situation where both parties have no option but to deal together, then withdrawal by one party is a very powerful manipulative technique. Some men use it almost as a way of life: they will not join in, they will walk away, show they do not care, and nothing—it seems—will make them. Countering the technique by providing strong leadership or using fierce criticism to draw them into a reaction might be successful.

To detect a manipulative intent means looking for signs of a behavioral lie. In some way, the words and actions will not ring true. If manipulation is suspected, then watch very carefully for signals given by the other party's non-verbal behavior.

It is very difficult for us to be fully competent behavioral liars. Actors and actresses are trained to it of course, and some people find it useful to develop a deliberately manipulative or deceptive technique for dealing with socially competitive situations. They then become trained to it. But always the sensitive person will know that *something* does not add up. Where an emotion is felt strongly then all of the reactions will be consistent with that emotion. The facial expression, the gestures, the posture, the body orientation, the speech patterns, all will reflect the internal emotion in a consistent way. It may be possible for us to control, for example, our facial expression or to use it to simulate anger, fear, shock-horror, etc. but to try and get all of them working together is too difficult for the ordinary man to accomplish. So where the signs are not consistent with the words, manipulation may be evident.

A certain amount of manipulation may be tolerated for a while. Perhaps a counter manipulative strategy may be deployed, and so for a time both parties are playing games which have little meaning. Often both parties realize what is going on, and they settle down to a sensible interaction.

But an end game may be necessary. This means that the negotiator brings the tactic out into the open and holds up the manipulative game itself to inspection. If the criticism is becoming unbearable and unjust, then at some point it will be useful to say: "Look, something is going on here which I don't quite understand. I have the feeling that something is wrong with this situation. If it goes on like this, then it will lead to nothing for either of us. Let us examine it..." and then the negotiator goes on to say what he suspects, but without attacking the other party directly, merely telling him how his actions are affecting him, the negotiator, adversely.

To bring out an issue of this kind does no harm. If it is not manipulative, then the other party will be at pains to demonstrate that his feelings are genuine — and he will modify his behavior also.

SUMMARY

The way in which the bargainer behaves is equally as important as the issues themselves. There may be times when it is necessary to display irritation or even anger, but in general the effective bargainer will ensure that he is to be trusted above all else. People must know that his word is good and that he will deliver his side of the bargain. Honesty about a proposition and its weaknesses will stand a bargainer in good stead, provided it does not reach the point of naivete. It is helpful if the bargainer is not only respected but is also liked personally. The personal touch by itself will not carry deals, but it will often carry the marginal deals against competition.

There is obviously an element of social deception involved in many deals; we may feign disinterest when we are in fact very excited, for example. We may also need to shape their behavior and condition them towards our way of thinking. We provide behavior signals to them, and their signals are useful to us. We may do some of our best deals through the use of third parties who can swing them in our favor. On the other hand, we ourselves will come up against manipulative behavior from time to time. We should watch for the signs of it, and expose it.

Mobilizing Bargaining Power | 5

Answer these questions both before *you read the chapter and* afterwards.

Q.1   *You are a world-famous Paris couturier. The annual showing of your new creations is to take place later in the week when the models, all free-lance, come to see you demanding an immediate increase in their fees. What do you do?*

(a) Talk with them together as a group; (b) talk with their leader, in your office; (c) talk with them one by one, in the workshop; (d) talk with them one by one later at your home by appointment.

Score   **Score**

——   ——

Before reading chapter.   *After reading chapter.*

——   ——

Q.2   *As part of your bargaining strength you want to build up your personal status so as to avoid being dominated by the other party.*
      Pick the correct status symbols:

(a) you wear Gucci shoes; (b) you offer them Superbowl tickets; (c) your wife wears best quality imitation pearls

Score   **Score**

——   ——

Before reading chapter.   *After reading chapter.*

——   ——

(d) you show them you are short of time because you are always busy; (e) you show them you have nothing to do; (f) you show you are in constant demand—people keep wanting to talk with you.

Score   **Score**

——   ——

Before reading chapter.   *After reading chapter.*

_____   _____

(g) *you have a personal assistant who flatters you;* (h) *you use a secretary to flatter you;* (i) *you do a little flattery of yourself.*

Score   **Score**

_____   _____

Before reading chapter.   *After reading chapter.*

_____   _____

(j) *you carry a smart briefcase;* (k) *your smart briefcase is carried for you;* (l) *you have no briefcase.*

Score   **Score**

_____   _____

Before reading chapter.   *After reading chapter.*

_____   _____

(m) *you are surrounded by people who do everything you ask;* (n) *you show your independence by doing things for yourself;* (o) *you allocate work tasks but handle your domestic affairs strictly by yourself.*

Score   **Score**

_____   _____

Before reading chapter.   *After reading chapter.*

_____   _____

(p) *you listen a lot;* (q) *you talk a lot;* (r) *you make jokes.*

Score   **Score**

_____   _____

Before reading chapter.   *After reading chapter.*

_____   _____

(s) *you arrange meetings with the other party in your office;* (t) ...*their office;* (u) ...*a place neutral to both parties.*

Score   **Score**

_____   _____

Before reading chapter.   *After reading chapter.*

_____   _____

Q.3   *A big government construction project in Sao Paulo is going wrong and it could threaten your company with huge costs. You need the assistance of one of the other big contractors to help you out. Their local chairman is supposed to be difficult to deal with. Do you:*

(a) go and see him; (b) discuss it with him on the telephone; (c) write to him first with the details of the problem?

Score   **Score**

_____   _____

Before reading chapter.   *After reading chapter.*

_____   _____

Q.4   *Later on, another smaller contractor needs your help in much the same way. Do you:*

(a) ask him to put his request on paper; (b) ask him to telephone you about it; (c) invite him to come and see you?

Score   **Score**

_____   _____

Before reading chapter.   *After reading chapter.*

_____   _____

Q.5   *You conduct seminars all over the world on your specialist subject, which is the anchoring of oil rig legs to sea beds over 500 fathoms deep. Oilmen sit devoutly at your feet. The Oilmen's Association of the North Atlantic has booked you to address their World Conference. They'll pay you in a bank account in Switzerland in one month's time. Do you:*

(a) insist on being paid in cash before you perform; (b) accept the payment into your Swiss bank; (c) leave the matter to them; (d) tell them it does not matter to you?

Score   **Score**

_____   _____

Before reading chapter.   *After reading chapter.*

_____   _____

Q.6   *Now you have been asked to speak to the Patagonian Deep Diving Association. Their organization to date has been very sloppy; you have made your own* *way to Patagonia at your expense because they failed to give you directions. When you arrive, only 20 people are there, and there is no other speaker except yourself. They have taken £250 from each delegate to come and hear you. You have the same options as in the previous question. What do you do?*

(a) (b) (c) (d)

Score   **Score**

_____   _____

Before reading chapter.   After reading chapter.

_____   _____

Q.7   *What should be the first move in persuading someone to do something:*

(a) *sell them the benefits;* (b) *answer their objections;* (c) *close them on the deal quickly;* (d) *identify the problem?*

Score   **Score**

_____   _____

Before reading chapter.   After reading chapter.

_____   _____

Mobilizing Bargaining Power | 5

The personal fortune of the thirty or so executives in the audience of top Malaysian businessmen could probably have paid for the building of the five-star Regent Hotel in Kuala Lumpur where this particular seminar was being held. These fortunes had been made by men who started with nothing, but who had deployed their skills in bargaining throughout their lives.

You could say, with breathless understatement, that these men were good at bargaining technique. They could spot an advantage at 8,000 miles, and take it.

One particular businessman was explaining how he and a few friendly competitors were taking advantage of a British multinational company which makes pharmaceutical and food and drink products. The time was early in 1975. The government in Britain—8,000 miles away—had imposed pricing restrictions upon companies such as this one. No British company was allowed to raise its prices in the UK market unless it had first obtained the permission of the government. It had to make out a case showing all the unavoidable cost increases, then discuss with negotiators from the Ministry who then generally refused to give their permission. However, British companies were allowed—indeed encouraged—to raise the prices of the goods they sold in overseas markets. This passed the problem on to foreigners, which did not matter because foreigners do not have a vote in British elections.

Here is a warning for all bargainers:

If you deal with governments, take care.
They don't fight fair.

As a result of this policy, companies made either smaller products or replaced the good quality material with cheaper substitutes. They often degraded their products in order to maintain their profits.

Bargainers should take one further note:

Companies don't fight fair either.

At the seminar, the Malaysian businessman was explaining how distributors could take advantage of British multinational companies. He was himself the boss of a supermarket chain. He had formed a buying ring with other supermarket operators and all of them were buying direct from an agent in the United Kingdom. By the time the products were landed in Port Kelang, the main

SELLER EXERCISING POWER

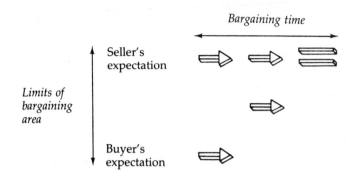

By holding firm, the seller is moving the buyer's expectations towards his own position.

BUYER EXERCISING POWER

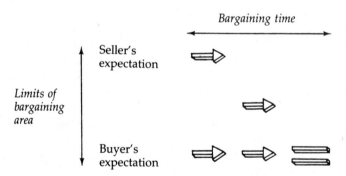

By holding firm, the buyer is gradually moving the seller's expectations toward his own. Because the bargaining room existed all the time, the seller could have moved the buyer and ended up with a better deal.

harbor of Malaysia, they were still 20% cheaper than the prices charged by the local factory which was owned by the British company. They were buying the smaller brand products in this way, not the market leaders which still came from the local factory source, being still cheaper than the imports.

The man nearest the market place nearly always has the edge. It is a feature of distribution practice all over the world that through the introduction of modern analysis and control systems built upon computers and micro-chips the power has moved from the hands of the supplier into the hands of the distributor.

One of the reasons why people are reading this book today is because of this shift in power. Last century the world was run by the people who could make things. But as more companies developed the technology of manufacturing, the competition became stronger. Then in the seventies the world started to slow down its consumption growth rate. This moved power into the hands of those with control of the market. This is why bargaining between buyer and seller is becoming more intractable and more difficult. The salesmen are losing their power base; the buyers are gaining. The alternative outlets for his goods and services are fewer for the salesman; the alternative sources willing to supply are wider for the buyer.

Paradoxically, this is also the reason why top salesmen become much more powerful inside their own organization during a recession. Because selling is so difficult then, and growth points so hard to find, the top sales negotiators can swing company policy their way. Salesmen are weaker, politically, during an expansionist phase.

The Malaysian supermarket chiefs had identified an alternative source of supply. Having alternatives is a key aspect of power. The local factory executives wanted to discuss the matter with them but they refused to admit to what they were doing. They did not want to enter into negotiations about it, so they used the technique of distancing themselves from the factory executives. Their distributors were always "out" when the telephone rang; they were never available for meetings; they asked for everything to be put in writing.

They wanted to maintain their bargaining power intact; by agreeing to a meeting they could only lose some of their power, or else they would cause a violent dispute with the company.

They had mobilized their power by getting together with their competitors. There is safety in numbers, and it increased the size and scope of the purchases they could make in London.

Bargaining is about the process of social exchange. In a book published in 1964 called *Exchange and Power in Social Life*, the author, Peter Blau, wrote: "The partner with fewer alternative opportunities tends to be more dependent upon and committed to the exchange relation than the other." And that describes the basis of bargaining power with precision.

The source of absolute power is one-sided dependence by one party upon the other. Where there is an element of interdependence, then such power is modified.

A person can establish his dominant position by overwhelming the other party with benefits, thereby increasing the obligations of the other party to him. Once this superiority is rooted in the structure of the relationship, then the dominant party can continue to extract benefits from the other party without damage to his superiority. In the old days, sellers were well on top when they dealt with a mass of relatively small buyers. Today nationalized concerns and government departments through their monopoly continue to assume what seems to be a "natural" authority over their many thousands of individual customers. But with shrinking markets, competitive suppliers, and with buyers grouped into very large and powerful buying units, it is the "natural" authority of the buyer which is now exerted.

The Malaysians were enjoying themselves, making money and proud of the fact that they could squeeze a British multinational giant. That was before they discovered themselves to be up to their necks in trouble.

They had played the game correctly. There was no breach of contract; on the other hand they did not go along to the company to ask permission.

Small hint for bargainers:

> *Never ask the question if you know you*
> *are not going to like the answer.*

They kept the company at arm's length and refused to come to the negotiating table. For the moment they were strong and the British factory was weak.

But you don't become a successful multinational company if you do not know a thing or two about power.

Large multinational companies making consumer products have a strong orientation towards the market. They hammer out their advertising and promotion campaigns behind an enormous amount of product development work in order to build themselves a market leadership position. Usually they will not enter a market segment unless they can see themselves becoming a leader in it. This gives them power. It is a lesson for all companies to follow.

The next round of the battle between the locally-based factory and the supermarket distributors took place two months after the seminar in which the Malaysians had been congratulating themselves on their shrewdness in pooling their orders and buying direct. This time the factory executives won hands down. Both sides ended up as good friends, and shook hands over the bargaining table. The Chinese Malaysians expect to win many of the bargaining games they play. But they are good losers, too, and they don't nurse revenge.

What the local factory did was to mess about with the deliveries and supplies of the products in which they were market leaders and which the supermarkets continued to buy. They withdrew in-store promotional support from the brands. The supermarkets had to sell to the public at full list price without offers and they were often out-of-stock.

Then the supermarkets found that the little shops all around them began to take huge slices of their regular trade away by making very deep price cuts and promotional offers on these very same brands. Their windows were plastered with large banners. The lines moved from the supermarket check-outs to the little shops who, for some strange reason, did not seem to experience any difficulty with the supply of products at all.

The supermarket buyers' ring collapsed and they all agreed to behave themselves once more. The story indicates one important factor about bargaining strategy. Most of the power display should be deployed outside the bargaining room and before the bargaining action starts. Do not make threats at this stage (don't make explicit threats at all, if possible). Just reveal your strength, indicate the power you have—but without threatening.

The purpose of bargaining strategy is to arouse the interest of the other party in your specific offering so that he can see few alternatives other than to accept your deal.

The assessment of bargaining power
It is vital to assess the relative bargaining power of both parties because this will determine the vigor, strength and direction of the demands.

In the second stage of the tussle between the Malaysian supermarket distributors and the local factory executives of the multinational company, after the supplies of the main product to the supermarkets had been withdrawn, the executives refused to deal with the supermarket bosses as one group. If they had done so, then they would have been pressured into concessions on margins, terms of trade, and the disputed area would have been widened. Instead, they picked off the supermarket bosses one by one, made appointments at their own factory offices and started with the weakest one first. Having broken him free from the ring, they then took on the others one by one, leaving the strongest until the last. By this time the strongest one was alone and worried. He capitulated willingly.

In any bargaining situation there is a reward offered to one party, which incurs him in an obligation to the other. Each party has a fundamentally simple choice, either to agree or not to agree.

The total bargaining situation is often extraordinarily complex. In theory many possibilities are open to either side to modify, amalgamate, or separate transactions. Negotiated settlements involve a myriad of exchanges, so that in essence, many bargains are involved before an overall settlement is reached.

In real life, bargainers usually consider few alternatives. The agile mind which can reconstruct a deal in a different way is a very rich asset. In this way, you can get them off their ground and on to yours.

Usually one party puts forward a propostion and argues for it strongly. If the other party works only within the proposer's frame of reference then he is running the risk of playing to the other man's rules. Better by far, to put forward a counter proposal, and to make the other party play to your rules. You can always go back to his game later. Meanwhile it cannot be a bad idea to test him out on your game first.

It can be noticed that in company sales forces, for example, the salesmen often seem to share the views and perceptions of the buyers with whom they work. In doing so, they often miss their own best arguments, some of which are never put to the buyers. The buyers are constantly forcing the salesmen down to a point of view where the competition seems stronger, and their own company weaker on all major issues.

There is a good hint for bargaining sellers in this:

> *Don't believe all that buyers tell you about your*
> *competitors' better quality and lower prices.*
> *They say these things because they are buyers.*

To assess your own bargaining power it is important to compare the results which will be obtained if:

(a) you agree with their proposition;
(b) you do not agree with their proposition.

(a) If you agree with their proposition, then what reward do you obtain, minus your corresponding obligations?

(b) If you do not agree with the propostion, then what chance have you of obtaining alternative rewards from another source and with what corresponding obligations?

If the costs of all kinds are greater than the benefits you can perceive, then your bargaining *power is strong*. This is because *you do not want the deal* as it stands at present. You would prefer an alternative deal, or no deal at all.

If the benefits you can perceive are higher than your costs, and the chance of realizing them is good, then your bargaining *power is weak* because *you want the deal*. Your overall power depends upon how much the other party wants the deal.

Notice that there is always a risk involved—there is always a chance that the other party might not make good his promises, or you cannot realize the advantages for some reason. Your colleagues might not agree with your assessment of the value of the deal. Notice also that your limits are set by the benefits you can *perceive*. It is the other party's duty to set up your expectations for his proposal, but at the same time he will try and close you off from looking for alternatives if he can. He will head you off from the difficulties. He will allow you to perceive only what he wants you to perceive. Equally, you are presenting your case to him in the same way, with the same intention.

Bargainers should ask themselves:

> *What does this guy know that I would be*
> *very interested in, if I knew it too?*

At the outset, it is also necessary to calculate the other party's bargaining power so far as this is possible.

The assessment of bargaining power between two parties cannot be measured with tidy calculations. Both parties are dealing with incomplete information about each other. Bargaining is as much based upon emotional preferences as on logic. So people tend to judge their relative bargaining power by the impressions they gain from the other party, his demeanor and behavior. In the end it is a matter of personal judgment. The relative power between the parties changes during the course of bargaining.

Bargaining power remains intact, absolutely, if no commitments are entered into. Whoever makes a concession, weakens his bargaining power slightly by indicating his need to accommodate the other party. But if neither side makes concessions, then no movement is possible and deadlock results.

To assess the other party's power, work out what they will lose if they do not do the deal with you; what alternatives they have available to them that *they* know about; and what they will have to give up if they do agree to the deal with you.

Compare this with your own position on these matters. Then you have the foundation for developing your bargaining strategy.

BARGAINING STRATEGY

Some men are hard—they hammer you down. Steven Enricott handles very large industrial accounts for audiovisual equipment. He recalls the time as a young man that he called on the purchasing officer for a group of hotels specializing in conference facilities. At the time they rented the equipment needed by their customers, but Steven wanted them to buy about six overhead projectors. He had prepared the case well. The buyer consistently refused him an appointment. Finally Steven told the secretary that he would wait all day if he had to. After half an hour the buyer saw him and opened with the words: "Whatever it is, I'm not interested in it. You can have three minutes, then I've got to go."

Steven closed up his bag and stood up. He said, "I'll go then, I quite understand if you are busy. Just so long as you know that the moment I step through that door you have lost $50,000."

The buyer had to call him back and listen to his story. They were now battling on equal terms. Steven had used a strategy to overwhelm the buyer with a benefit, a strategy which he had worked out in advance, but he expressed the benefit in the form of *losses to the buyer*.

He, and thousands of salesmen all over the world, have used similar strategies to make men listen and to arouse their interest. The unfortunate thing is that these salesmen are outnumbered by those who do not even realize that such problems can be handled. Many of them do not get past the secretary.

There is a caution in this for bargainers:

Remember a secretary may be a member of the bargaining team.

In developing bargaining strategy there are four aspects to note:

BARGAINING POWER
BARGAINING TIME
BARGAINING DISTANCE
BARGAINING MANEUVER

Bargaining from strength

An exhibition of naked power can be very frightening. The man who seeks domination over others is helped if he has a warm approach and is sociable.

Many organizations and many people will refuse to deal with those who by reputation make tough demands, or exercise their power in a brutal way.

People are always apprehensive of very large buyers—so when operating from a position of strength it is essential to make the necessary self-effacing overtures to draw them to the bargaining table.

The other party needs encouragement; later and gradually his expectations must be carefully lowered, but this should be done in such a way as to prevent him withdrawing.

The other party also needs to win something from the negotiations; something which he can carry home in triumph to his own camp. The astute strong bargainer will apparently fight hard on some issue which the other, weaker, party wants badly, and will then make a concession. Concessions should not all be one-way, just because one party is strong. It is important to let the others win, too. That is why collaborative bargaining has been called a "Win–Win" game.

The man who is nervous will not open up, nor will he reveal himself, his hopes and his fears. So the stronger party may have to deliberately reduce his power in order to get the other man to relax and to open up.

A substantial textile manufacturing company of world renown controls its subsidiary operations through budgets. These are discussed with the chief executive of each division and selected members of company management. In any company these are always difficult meetings. Because the company wants the divisional chiefs to feel relaxed and at ease, they hold the meetings at the offices of the divisional executives, and do not call the chief executives to the head office. By deliberately moving to the other man's territory, he is made more confident, and they feel that they achieve a discussion and decision of higher quality as a result.

Bargaining from weakness

Here everything possible should be done before the start to build up the strength of the position such as it is. Alternative prospects need to be sought for whatever is being offered; the maximum amount of research and information is required in order to identify the other party's pressure points.

At all costs, the weakness of the bargainer's position must not be revealed by word or deed to the other party. If this mistake is made, then the bargainer is in danger of being pressed by the other party to make every concession possible and will be forced down to the lower limit of his expectations. Only if he is faced by a weak or unskilled opposite number or when the cost of the deal to the other party is not high in relation to his resources will he get away with the error of revealing his need.

The bargainer's strength, such as it is, should be reinforced—small things will help. Getting the other party on to your own territory, your own factory or office, will help provided that the surroundings will help your status. Using personal assistants, wearing high-status clothes, making certain that you are seen to be powerful perhaps by having nothing apparently to do (kings never look busy), even the fact that you tend to listen rather than to talk a lot—all of this helps to increase your power.

If you can demonstrate interest but not eagerness in the other party's proposition, then that is a help. Your object must be to get the other party walking towards you—you must be prepared to take a risk and walk away.

If you are weak, then increase the informality between the parties. Meet the other party face to face, and secure a warm personal relationship with him.

You must be prepared to use pressure tactics at any stage in the process. You can wear the other party down. You can sow confusion and doubt about the other party's case.

Probably your most valuable weapon during the course of bargaining is persistence-and-dedication to the aim, without overselling. The man who is likable, insistent in a courteous way, and keeps going relentlessly for what he wants wins a great many deals that other men would lose. Fatigue and despair lose many men their results; they just let the other party slip away.

Bargainers take special note:

> *Many a weak case has been won at 3:00 a.m. from the wreckage*
> *of tiredness and a hangover.*

The assessment of power is based upon personal judgment of these factors and does not lend itself to fine calculations. If a man is eager to do business with you, then he is seen to be weak and you are strong. The paradox of human nature is that we tend to want that which we cannot have.

Take, for example, this case of an inventor who felt that he had to go out and "sell" his product hard. In doing so, he came close to bankruptcy, until he discovered that the art of marketing as opposed to the art of selling is to make them come marching to your door. It was this discovery of his, not the discovery of his invention, which was to make him rich.

There is a small electronics company run by a top electronics engineer. He invented a measuring device which was suitable for many applications in different industries. He went out to sell it. He produced leaflets about it, he went to see the big companies and generally had a hard time getting it all going. He invented other products for other markets and experienced no more success than with the first. So he took stock. He remembered the maxim of a previous boss who had said to him, "Get into a market where they need what you have, dedicate yourself to that market, and be the biggest in it." So he altered the strategy.

Instead of chasing after the buyers himself, he organized small demonstrations of his equipment in hotels around the country. He invited the important technical chiefs in the area to come to the hotel, he set his men out in cars to pick them up, and he gave them a buffet luncheon and some wine. In the demonstrations he shocked his staff by saying that he only took orders for six at a time. Soon, the enquiries started to come through from the purchasing officers. People asked to come and see him and to see his factory. The word of his devices spread. They were written up in the trade papers, and business developed well.

His staff wanted him to expand and to develop other products but he refused. Instead of expanding his production capacity he put up his prices. His products became fairly rare and expensive, and he went on improving them.

In the end a large competitor entered his market. But he had his reputation established. His prices are still high. And he still outsells everyone else.

Timing

Having a sense of timing is a vital requirement for the negotiator. Judge the moment right, offer a spectacularly good deal, and you might catch all the opposition off its guard by a "Quick Thrust." This is where your offer is too good for them to miss. This is where your first offer is your last offer, and you put a closure on the deal. Impose a deadline at the time you make the offer. *"This is an unrepeatable deal at half the normal cost and we will hold it open to you for twenty-four hours. You must take it or leave it by then."*

Otherwise you may have to be patient over a prolonged exchange, taken over many different sessions. It is not always possible, but it is usually better to have more time available than the other man, so that ultimately the pressure to close is upon him.

A sense of timing is needed also for obtaining movement during the bargaining sessions. Many hours may be spent in boring technical discussion or in other exchanges of information. One party or the other may need jogging to keep the momentum going, but movement only becomes possible when both parties sense the moment is right.

The important factor is to calculate in advance whether any delay is going to work in your favor or in favor of the other party. Can you structure their expectations so that they perceive the deal operating within a certain time scale which suits them? Then you can keep them moving to this point.

Dead men, they say, tell no tales. In this example one company was in dispute with another. The other party needed one of its executives to be a witness if the matter ever came to court. But the fact that this executive was to leave the company to work overseas was known to the first company. They therefore structured their bargaining strategy around the advantage of timing.

A Danish paint company had a contract to supply a Copenhagen shipyard with marine paint for several new boats. The negotiations went wrong at the end when one of the boat orders was cancelled. The president of the paint company was holding out for the full cost of all the paint supplied, while the shipyard wanted to return a substantial amount. The shipyard was claiming that their engineering chief had privately agreed to the return of the paint with the sales chief of the supplier, so they refused to pay the bill.

Normally, the supplier should chase very hard on the account because delay in this kind of dispute will nearly always work in the customer's favor because he holds the money and refuses to pay. This will eventually wear down the supplier. But on this occasion they did not press hard, they let the matter lie for a while. They knew the shipyard engineer was to leave the company to take a job abroad in the Far East. Once he had left, then the shipyard had no documentation and no witnesses to the discussion. The shipyard did not realize the game which was to be played, otherwise they could have had their engineer sign a statement. Once he had left, it was too late.

The engineer left, the shipyard was taken to court and the two companies settled the issue outside the courtroom door.

Take the question of credit terms, for example. Some customers have a sound reputation and credit may be freely allowed by the suppliers. Others, however, may be sensed to be bad debt risks. The bills must be paid by these customers before the goods are delivered: it is fatal to wait until afterwards, because the power relationship has changed afterwards. You might not get your bill paid at all.

With a delay, levers may become available to one party or the other. Bargaining power changes with time.

The point is that circumstances change. Many bargaining situations have been started under one set of assumptions, only to end up with a totally different deal from that which was planned originally, simply because the entire circumstances have changed.

Distance

To build up your bargaining power you must get close to the other party. From a position of weakness, where you know very little about him and his needs, you will have difficulty in establishing your objectives. Under these circumstances you will need to increase the personal influence you can bring to bear.

Suppose you are having a little difficulty with your personal income tax. The taxman is saying that you owe the government rather more than you think you owe. The first advice to you is to use an accountant to sort out your matters for you. Let an expert deal with another expert. But suppose you do not choose this course, what then? Do not deal with the situation by correspondence whatever you do. This is playing the other party's game. Go and see them, talk to them. You may surprise yourself and find that they are perfectly reasonable people who are only too pleased to see their "clients." It is a lonely job being a taxman. They are only too happy for a bit of company now and then. You can satisfy this need of theirs and in exchange they will help you over your tax problem. No—they really will, however much you may doubt it.

The problem is that you may have built up a stereotype in your mind of a grasping, difficult taxman. They are no more like that than the average salesman is a loud-mouthed, aggressive bore. One or two may be so, but the vast majority are not like that at all. (On the other hand, if you are yourself a tax collector, it will generally pay you to conduct affairs by correspondence. Keep them at arm's length, otherwise you will only end up making concessions to them.)

Local government authorities are often quoted as being among the most difficult buyers with whom to deal. They use their buying power to force suppliers to submit written quotations without previous meetings, and the lowest quotes win. If you are a contractor doing local construction projects, your prices must be keen, and it is difficult to escape from the system.

But suppliers do not usually realize that the bargaining is often all over by the time their quotation has been submitted. The thing to do is to obtain meetings with local officials well in advance of the specifications being drawn up, and to persuade them to draw up the specifications in such a way that only your organization can meet them. That is not possible for everyone; but many companies do exactly this.

What they do is to try to maximize the informality of the relationship; they get to know the people personally. Sometimes, they get into local politics and have themselves elected on to local boards themselves. There is no corruption implied in this, but it cannot be damaging to their business to be well known and liked by all the board members, to be able to help them out here and there, and to make sure that a few favors are exchanged in return.

Distance is an important part of bargaining strategy, when married up to timing. There are times when it pays to maintain one's position intact by refusing to meet the other party.

When you are uncertain of the situation, doubtful about the outcome and in a weak bargaining position, then get as close to them at all levels as you can.

Using the telephone is less sociable and much less effective in winning concessions than a face-to-face meeting. At a face-to-face meeting the stronger party is nearly always obliged to make a concession, which he will not do on the telephone.

On the other hand, when it pays you to maintain your strength, then hold them off and use delay. Get them to put it all in writing. That commits them, but does not commit you.

If you know that you are strong, then gently let them know in some way. Bargainers can take a lesson from a plumber's advertisement in a New York newspaper:

"When you need a plumber, you need a plumber."

Maneuver

Four strategic bargaining maneuvers can be identified:

COERCION
INDUCEMENT
EDUCATION
PERSUASION

The first two maneuvers are often used by strong buyers, while the last two are used more often by sellers.

The coercive strategy is used by those with strong bargaining power and is particularly disliked by the other party who is forced to comply. If conflict bargaining is involved, where both parties are locked in and must deal together as in many industrial disputes, or commercial disputes, or in monopoly supplier and buyer relationships, then the use of this technique is likely to cause a desire for revenge by the other party. This subsequent revenge can take very unpleasant forms, because it will be applied in stealth and will be designed to cause the maximum amount of disruption and embarrassment to the party who used the leverage originally.

A particularly unpleasant man ran a small food processing business. He was renowned throughout his trade for his autocratic style and arrogant manner—to his customers, to his staff, to everyone with whom he came into contact, in fact. The only problem was that he was very good at his business—so good that he had rubbed out most of the opposition.

He employed his nephew, who grew to detest him. Later, upon some pretext, he fired his nephew. On his way out of the factory, the youngster took a hose pipe and sprayed water for ten minutes upon half a ton of yeast. Yeast ferments. It fermented its way into the computer room. The young man was inundated with job offers from delighted competitors and from customers who heard the story.

Some negotiators have been known to steal what they want, others use force, threats of legal action, threats of commercial disruption, industrial disruption, and so on.

The coercive maneuver is usually counter-productive and is to be avoided. On the other hand, from time to time it will be used against you, and you yourself may need it to force movement from the other party.

If you have to use force then do so unexpectedly and heavily, so that they cannot counter-attack. Then, when they are expecting the worst give them a chance to move in your direction without losing face. They will usually move. But remember that some people will counter-attack even when it is plainly not in their interest to do so. Such people will go down fighting whatever the odds stacked against them. Such is the stuff of martyrs. So never attack potential martyrs. And never, ever, threaten an attack if you do not mean to go through with it. Your bluff is likely to be called and you will then be in deep trouble.

Inducement

This maneuver seeks to give the other party something of value which he wants badly and which is sufficient to overcome the other party's resistance to the rest of the deal. The inducement changes the balance of the whole transaction so that the other party sees that it is in his interest to settle. Paying a premium, offering a bonus or gift, added services, extra product, the promise of long-term business, offering a special discount—all these actions and many more can be listed as inducements.

An *educative* maneuver is one that is designed to change the broad attitudes and beliefs of the other party, thereby producing a favorable response. It can be very expensive and very difficult to alter completely a "set" of values held by another party. It cannot be done by information supply alone. The process is so similar to the process of persuasion that we can deal with them both together.

Persuasion

A persuasive maneuver is one that obtains its results through identifying the natural interests of the other party with the transaction. The appeal can be to the other party's sense of logic—by the presentation of figures perhaps. Or it can be an appeal to his emotions—by painting a picture of the future perhaps. Or it can be an appeal to his sense of value—demonstrating the overall appropriateness of the deal.

Here is an eight-step approach to persuasion, which you will find to be effective. It is not the only way of doing the job, but it is the best way.

1. Get to the *problem* first. Make sure he can identify, describe and if possible measure the cost of his problem. You may have to make him see one. The benefits of your proposition do not help at this stage, until he sees them in terms of opportunities for himself. The problem can only be found through asking probing questions.

2. Agree on the *solution* next. Work with him and secure his agreement to the lines of your general proposal which will solve his problem. Shape his responses in your direction, by encouraging his remarks when they favor your line of approach and by withdrawal or resistance if he raises objections.

3. Select the key *benefits*. Select only the benefits to him of your propostion which will fit the solution you have outlined. Do not describe more benefits than are necessary at this stage. The more your complete hand is revealed, the weaker your position. You will need other benefits held in reserve to counter his resistance.

4. Supply *proofs* of what you say. This is a very important stage. Give him evidence, charts, figures, graphs, drawings, pictures, test results, third party references, research data to back up what you claim—particularly when you make claims about the quality of your services. It is no good saying "Ours is the best." You have to describe in what way it is the best, and you have to supply some evidence to back up your claim. Otherwise he is going to think to himself: "I've heard all of this before."

5. Secure his *agreement*. Make sure that he comes with you; if he back-tracks and resists, go back to the problem. You should insure his agreement before the next stage.

6. Minimize his *cost*. Spread the cost thin; compare it to something else small; show it extended over time; break up the cost into small chunks; do not hesitate, but go immediately to the next stage.

7. Give him one *additional* benefit. This should be introduced immediately after the statement of cost.

8. Finally, sum up his *profits*. Summarize your entire case so far, and together with him work out his gross profit; accumulate this over a long time ahead.

BARGAINING POWER TACTICS AND PLAYS

In the following chapters, which all concern the actual operation of the bargaining process, a series of the more common tactics and plays have been included.

Many of these tactics can be used at various stages of the process and they come in many guises. In general they have been included at the end of the chapter which seems most appropriate for them.

To illustrate how each play works, a case is imagined where Mr. Sells is selling his house to a Mr. Purchase. Sometimes Mr. Agent is involved and sometimes other characters enter the scene. In a house buying and selling situation where third parties are involved, a rich vein of opportunities for different tactics is afforded to the bargainer. The choice of a house purchase example is made in order to provide a constant frame of reference for each tactic and play, and because the example is familiar to many of us. Most readers will recall examples of the use of these tactics and plays in their business life. They are part and parcel of the gaming process—each is captioned with a sports metaphor.

Look what a star player I am
Watch out for the other party's high-status signals; his big car, his plush office, his good address, his chauffeur, his wall-to-wall secretaries, his personal press publicists. They are all designed to put him up and you down. Two kinds of people use such status symbols to build their power. Genuine stars and genuine crooks.

"Would you do me the personal favor of popping into my apartment when you are in town, then I can give you the key to my daughter's house, if you are still interested in buying it," says Mr. Sells. "Perhaps you would then let me buy you a drink, or perhaps you would have a bite with me if you come at lunchtime."

"Certainly, I'd like to. Where do you live?"

"Suite 15, top floor, The Plaza."

The response you should give to this? Eccentricity has status too. "Is there someone there who can look after my bike?"

Kick off the game when they are not looking?
The man who starts before the other is looking has an enormous advantage. He can creep up on his opposite number, research the situation, prepare his case and put himself in a dominant position immediately.

Mr. Purchase does not call immediately on Mr. Sells when he wants to buy his house. He calls on his neighbors, he looks at the local school, local shops, he surveys other similar properties in the district and obtains comparative prices. Then, armed with this information, he makes his move. Every benefit outlined by Mr. Sells is countered with a weakness. Mr. Purchase has control, because he has information.

What should be done to counter the well-informed party? Ask him the questions, don't make statements. Keep the conversation loose until he has revealed most of what he knows.

Buy our program

The man who arranges the agenda for the meeting has a control upon the decisions. He can ensure that only those topics which he wishes to include for discussion are included. Be careful if they produce their own program for the game: this will build their power.

Mr. Agent sends you a questionnaire since you are searching for properties in the area. How important is it for you, he wants to know, to have four/five bedrooms, large garden, school nearby, other facilities, etc.? Ostensibly, he argues that this will help him to match you with exactly the right property. But he will use the information to help him sell you any house he wants to get rid of. He knows what to concentrate upon and what your weak points are. He will take you around several properties and point out only those features which he knows will appeal to you.

The counter to this? Send him your own program first.

We are only amateurs, really

Watch this sneaky tactic. The purpose of this self-effacing approach is to make you relax and think you have got an easy game ahead. It is designed to secure your sympathy. It does not look like a power play, but it is.

"We feel awful, we've never bought a house before," says Mr. Purchase. "Would you mind if the children scrambled all over the place? They're so excited you see. Is my wife in the kitchen already? Goodness, this is all so new to us. Tell me, what sort of questions should I be asking you?"

Before long he will have you telling him the problems with the house as well as the benefits; your wife will tell his wife about the noisy children in the neighborhood, and, worst of all, you'll end up showing him the tiny upstairs attic, last of all. (You should make sure he sees it, first of all, to get it out of his memory.)

To counter this ploy—you have never sold a house before either, have you?

Time wasting: or, I don't really want to play

This is a nasty little power gambit. When you are all ready to start, then they put you off. They indicate they are probably not interested after all. A strong version of the same tactic is to tell you they have had a change of mind. The intention is to see if you will still come after them; if so, they have weakened your position and you may offer some early concessions in order to arouse their interest.

Mr. Sells says, on the telephone, "I don't know whether we are doing the right thing really. I personally want to sell, but my wife and children love this place. So do I, come to that. I don't know what to do, what do you think?"

He is now forcing you, the buyer, so persuade him to sell. He is reversing the roles. If you do go after him, then he will hold out for his full demand and he can always claim later, "I am only doing this to please you." It may be genuine, and if you want the deal you will have to go after him. Later on, though, when his interest is higher, you can back off yourself, saying that you wish you hadn't persuaded him now, and that he must make up his own mind. It could pay to lose the initial skirmish, in order to win the battle later.

SUMMARY

Power is based upon the damage which will result if the parties do not agree. If one party is likely to suffer no effective damage, while the other will lose out badly, then the first party is strong and the second is weak. The source of this question has to do with the quality and range of options available to each party in the event of the deal breaking down.

From a weak position, the strength must be built up to equalize with the other as far as possible. Much of this work should be done beforehand. Weakening the other party, by criticism perhaps, will strengthen the relative power of the bargainer.

Persuasion is only one of the strategies to be deployed. But we can also seek to educate the other party in a very broad fashion; or we can coerce them if we have some hold over them, or we can add some extra inducement for them to accept our deal.

Timing is important; the power relationship changes over time. Keeping one's distance is another important factor in retaining strength.

It is possible to be too strong though—the other party may be nervous and may seek to withdraw. In this case it may pay to weaken the position somewhat, in order to relax the other party.

* * *

Now go back to the questionnaire at the start of this chapter and complete it again.

Setting Up the Deal | 6

Before reading this chapter, fill in the answers to these questions. Then, after you have read the chapter, fill in the answers again. You can then look up your scores at the end of the book.

Your boat is powered by a Mercury outboard engine, 20 h.p. bought in 1975. According to a published engine price guide it should now be worth about $700 at retail price (from a dealer) including the extras. It includes an electric start, control box and gas tank. You have it serviced twice a year at $150 a time and it is very reliable, but it is getting rather old and this worries you. You fancy buying a Yahama engine to replace it—the dealer is near your boat mooring, but he has a reputation for high prices in a market characterized by cut-price offers. The list price retail for the new electric start Yamaha plus box and tank is $1,720. The market is depressed and it is the start of the selling season. If you take off whatever you will get for your Mercury from what you think you will have to pay for the Yamaha, what is likely to be your net outlay for the new engine? At present you have no other information.

Circle the figures chosen

Q.1 *The best deal you think you might achieve*

a	b	c	d	e	f
$900–999	$1,000–1,099	$1,100–1,199	$1,200–1,299	$1,300–1,399	$1,400–1,499

Q.2 *The worst possible deal you would accept*

a	b	c	d	e	f
$900–999	$1,000–1,099	$1,100–1,199	$1,200–1,299	$1,300–1,399	$1,400–1,499

Q.3 *The deal you expect to do*

a	b	c	d	f
$900–999	$1,000–1,099	$1,100–1,199	$1,200–1,299	$1,300–1,399	$1,400–1,499

Q.4 *What is your objective for the deal at this stage, before you start buying and selling?*

a	b	c	d	e	f
$900–999	$1,000–1,099	$1,100–1,199	$1,200–1,299	$1,300–1,399	$1,400–1,499

Score   **Score**

___

Before reading chapter.   *After reading chapter.*

___

Q.5   *How do you approach your chosen Yamaha agent?*
(a) *Offer him the Mercury as a trade-in?* (b) *ask him for his best price for the Yamaha?* (c) *tell him your problem and ask for his advice?* (d) *do not approach him, but approach other agents first for their offers?*

Score   **Score**

___

Before reading chapter.   *After reading chapter.*

___

Q.6   *New Yamahas of the kind you want are being advertised by discount dealers at the price of $1,380, excluding delivery. You go to your local Yamaha dealer and tell him what you are prepared to pay in cash, showing him the competitive quotations. Do you:*
(a) *ask him for his best price?* (b) *tell him that since you can buy one for $1,380, there is no reason to pay more?* (c) *ask him what he feels about $1,340?*

Score   **Score**

___

Before reading chapter.   *After reading chapter.*

___

Q.7   *He refuses absolutely to discount his engine to you at a price below $1,500, pointing out that this price includes the initial service, free delivery and fitting, and a service-backed guarantee. "You try to get something fixed afterwards by these cut-price types," he says. "You don't know where these cut-price engines have come from." He will not take your Mercury in part-exchange, but offers to put it on display for you and sell it second-hand acting as agent only, without giving his own guarantee. He thinks you might get $400 for it perhaps. But you will have to take the Yamaha at $1,500. He tells you he has only this one in stock. Incidentally his service to you will be cheap because your boat is nearby and his mileage charge will be low, he points out.*
(a) *Do you take the deal?* (b) *do you go away and think about it?* (c) *do you refuse completely to entertain the idea?* (d) *do you tell him that you can afford only a net $1,999 because that is the limit of your savings?*

Score   **Score**

_____   _____

       Before reading chapter.   *After reading chapter.*

_____   _____

Q.8   *You then have a brainwave. The agent for Mercury engines is also close by. The Mercury list prices are practically identical to Yamaha, and the cut-price offers from discounters are also identical. Mercury engines are just as good as Yamaha. What deal do you propose to the Mercury dealer? (Write out the features of your propostion; you will score marks for each good feature you include. Which arguments will persuade him to do the deal with you? How will you price your demands?)*

Score   **Score**

_____   _____

       Before reading chapter.   *After reading chapter.*

_____   _____

Q.9   *The Mercury agent says he does not think he can make the deal you want but he can offer you a year-old second-hand Mercury engine cheap, and would you consider that? Alternatively he has a 15 h.p. engine he can sell to you which is new, but is a bit less powerful than the one you want. Do you:*
   (a) discuss his suggestions; (b) say nothing; (c) get him back to your deal; (d) walk out with nothing decided, saying you will think about it all?

Score

_____

Q.10 *To get the best deal, should you now try and complete: (a) quickly; (b) slowly; (c) it does not matter?*

Score   **Score**

_____   _____

       Before reading chapter.   *After reading chapter.*

_____   _____

Q.11 *When he refuses your suggestions should you:*
   (a) persist with your ideas; (b) change them around a bit; (c) ask him for his alternative suggestions; (d) reduce your demands?

Score   **Score**

———

Before reading chapter.   *After reading chapter.*

———

Setting up the Deal | 6

Women can be very hard bargainers, when they go to the limit to obtain what they want.

Equally, to get to the top in politics, in any country, you have to be tough and determined. Governments are made of hard people.

So when a woman becomes Prime Minister in the world's oldest major democracy, you can expect some exceptional things to happen. In December 1979, in Dublin, they did.

When the Heads of Governments within the EEC meet, there is a protocol established to which they all conform. They are courteous to each other, deferential almost, and they disguise their inner steel with charm. Mrs. Thatcher, as the head of the British Government, was presenting them with a problem. She thought that her country was paying too much towards the Community budget. Because of a bias in the way the budget contributions were levied, her case was that Britain was putting in much more than she was getting out by way of benefits. She argued her case strongly and asked for a reduction of about £1 billion a year in Britain's contribution. The answering smiles on the faces of the other EEC Premiers were shortly to become frozen. They offered her £250 million and thought that would be almost the end of the matter.

At this stage, the bargaining area had become established. The EEC Premiers offered the £250 million, knowing that after a hard discussion, they might have to go up to £300 million. That would not be offered initially, but that figure was about their expectation level.

The British Government knew this, from advance soundings in the capitals of Europe. They knew that in a bargaining situation they must always ask for more than they expect go get. That is the rule, and there are few exceptions to it.

Bargaining is about each party making an initial demand or offer, receiving a counter offer, and then the two parties moving towards a final agreement somewhere in the middle.

There is very little opportunity for a bargainer to obtain a result which is higher than the demand he makes at first. Once the opening demand is on the table, the bargainer can only retreat from this position; he cannot get more.

He may be playing a long-term strategy of course, whereby he develops a small deal with his opposite number initially, knowing that later he is going to

wind him up to a bigger deal—but this is an exception to the rule that bargainers should always ask for more than they expect go get.
Tip for sellers:

> *If you want him to give you an order for thirty,*
> *ask him to take forty.*

Once the opening demand has been made, then the other party is free to move towards the other end of the scale. The initial demands are now some way apart. It is the task of each party to move the other one towards their own limit.
Tip for buyers:

> *If you plan to take thirty, see what*
> *he'll offer you for an order of twenty.*

Two things have now happened. First the bargaining area has been established. Secondly, each party now has a set of private expectations about the outcome of the deal. These expectations are not set at the limit of the opening demands because both parties know that bargaining room exists. But whatever vague aspirations existed previously, they are now beginning to firm up.

One aim of bargaining is to alter the other party's expectations to your level. It is only when both parties' final sets of expectations are in line with one another, that a deal is possible.

The EEC Premiers were quite confident that they would be able to settle the British demand at around £300 million off the British payments, because experience had taught them that matters were usually settled amicably in this way. But they forgot they were dealing with a very resolute woman, one who did not want to play the game by the rules of their club. She had her own rules and she was going to force them to play her game.

Before Mrs. Thatcher went to the Dublin Conference she knew that, barring a miracle, there would be deadlock ensuing. She would cause it by setting a very high demand, sticking to it unmercifully, and that she would be changing the rules of debate. First, she presented the logical case which added up to her claim for £1 billion. She then called this sum "Britain's money" and went on calling it this despite the extreme irritation this caused to the other premiers, particularly those of France, Germany, and Denmark—the first two countries would have the most to lose if the budgetary rules were altered.

An ugly scene ensued. Instead of the ritual by which both parties move gently towards each other, both parties stood their ground. The demands were too far apart. With a demand set at £1 billion facing an offer of £250 million, the two parties had lost contact with each other. Deadlock resulted and no agreement was reached.

To experience deadlock early in the discussions may be no bad thing. When the other party's demands are too strong, when they use force and power, then you must walk away. If you stay talking, they will overwhelm you. You will be hammered to your lowest point.

But if you walk away, you are showing your independence. You are showing you do not need them. You are showing how strong you are. If they want you they will come after you; their demands will be modified. You will have altered their expectations.

You must get the timing right, however. They must be interested in what you have to offer them, when you create the deadlock. Otherwise, they might let you keep on walking.

Helpful hint for bargainers:

> *Walking out will show them how strong you are.*
> *But it won't help if you have to go crawling back.*

It now became the duty of each party in turn to convince the other to alter his expectations. In the EEC dispute threat signals were now made to each side. Mrs. Thatcher told the House of Commons that Britain would "play by the

---

SELLERS' BARGAINING OBJECTIVES

"There is something wrong here.
Why does he want my deal so badly?"

Desirable objective
limit

— — — — — — — — .

Acceptable
objective limit

Mandatory
objective limit

Best possible
deal for him and
usual limit of
opening demand

The deal he
expects

Worst possible
deal for him

"I prefer no deal at all. The offer
is not high enough."

(a)

---

rules of the EEC." This implied that there was a choice and was a warning signal to the other countries. It also added pressure to one of the leading proponents on the other side, the French, who were at the time breaking the EEC laws by banning the importation of British lamb.

The French responded with a threat signal of their own. Their newspapers began to print stories about how Britain might resolve the issue by accepting a new lower grade of membership in the EEC—a sort of associate status. The French have always known how to twist the knife in the British psyche.

Changing the other party's expectations can be very difficult indeed. In some way, the other party must come to realize that he is not going to achieve all that he wants. If the other party is firmly committed to his ambitions, if his fears and hopes for the issue are tied up with his aims for a good result, then you will be trampling on his emotions. The more he is committed to his aim, the greater will be his disappointment. That is why great care is needed at this stage. You must fly kites, you must pass signals, you must give them all kinds of indications and assistance to lower their sights.

If the aims of two determined bargainers are far apart and they each remain determined, then the resulting clash of wills can be fierce. They may each withdraw from the bargaining table, and stay apart. If they are in a conflict

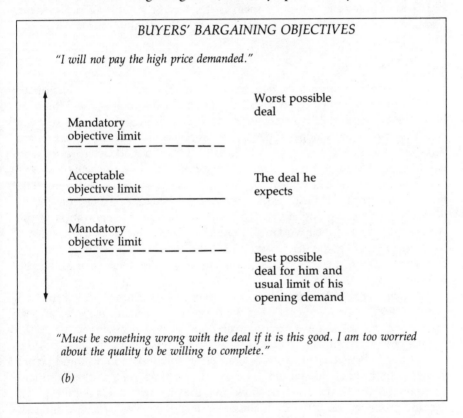

BUYERS' BARGAINING OBJECTIVES

"I will not pay the high price demanded."

Worst possible deal

Mandatory objective limit

Acceptable objective limit

The deal he expects

Mandatory objective limit

Best possible deal for him and usual limit of his opening demand

"Must be something wrong with the deal if it is this good. I am too worried about the quality to be willing to complete."

(b)

bargaining situation where both parties have to continue to work together and they must come to a decision, then great pressure and coercion will be used. This is the source of strikes, lock-outs, demonstrations, picketing, and of much private violence in society.

It is easy also for such violence to become naturally a part of the bargaining routine so that it becomes expected. Each year, around November, the transport workers' unions in Great Britain agree new wage rates for the drivers of oil tankers. The bargaining is always "heavy" and the unions take on each oil company in turn. But each year they start the negotiating round with a different major oil company. This first round nearly always results in a dispute which is followed by industrial action. Gasoline is not delivered to the chosen company's service station customers. Their other oil company rivals pick up the business. So the chosen company collapses, and concedes more than it would like to. Then it establishes a "norm" for the settlements that year in the industry which is then followed by each of the other companies in turn, usually without industrial action. The later agreements are resolved very quickly after the first.

The point is that the unions pick a different company every year with whom to deal first. The entire game has become ritualized. The companies concerned even know in advance which of them is due for the trouble. The force, the coercion, has been built into the structure of the bargaining routine.

THE BARGAINING AREA

At the start of the process three different bargaining objectives can be identified. The first of them is what could be called the "best deal"—that is, the fulfillment of all the hopes of the bargainer in every sense. This represents the best for which he can possibly hope. When, for example, construction contractors are very busy and can take on no more work, they have a tendency to price new work deliberately high so that they will not get it. Although this will turn most customers away, some customers will accept those outrageous quotations. The builders then try to fit in the extra work as best they can, flitting from job to job, keeping several going at the same time, to the intense aggravation of the customers, who find their workmen popping off in the middle of a job to work somewhere else. The builders have landed the new work at the maximum of their expectations, their "best deal" level, and it therefore pays them to handle it if they can.

The next bargaining objective is lower than this. It could be called the "acceptable deal." This represents what the bargainer anticipates to be a fair deal for himself. He asked for more originally, but did not really expect to get it. He has ended up with more or less what he thought he would get from the deal. It pays a bargainer to have this limit firmly established in his mind before he goes into the bargaining room. If he accepts anything less than this he should be disappointed. All the evidence shows that the man who holds out for a high demand firmly will do better deals altogether than the one who is uncommitted in his own mind to what he wants. The construction contractor must run his business on the basis of getting a standard rate of return for his work, and the majority of his deals must be done at this "acceptable" rate.

The reason so many contractors go bankrupt is that they allow themselves to be pressed down to their lower limit too often. They are too ready to accept deals at their "worst deal" level. This is the lowest the bargainer will accept; he would rather withdraw from the deal altogether than accept a worse result than this. To accept the deal at this level must represent great disappointment. The deal falls well short of his original hopes, and even falls short of his expectations.

THE BARGAINING AREA

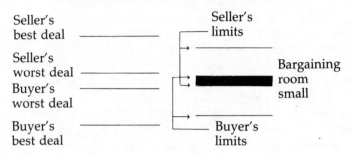

Seller's best deal ——————

Seller's worst deal ——————

Buyer's worst deal ——————

Buyer's best deal ——————

Seller's limits

Bargaining room small

Buyer's limits

NO DEAL

No deal is possible here. There is no bargaining room. What the seller wants is far more than the buyer is expecting to give.

A deal cannot be done until both parties have altered the expectations of the other.

POOR DEAL

A deal is possible here because there is some bargaining room. But neither party is realizing its acceptable objective. Each one will search for alternative opportunities of doing a better deal before they agree to this one. This will be a long and protracted debate, with much aggravation and disappointment. Two hard bargainers, both of them determined people, are likely to be unable to agree on this deal.

Seller's → —————— limits

Buyer's limits

A GOOD DEAL

Here a successful deal is entirely possible. Both parties can get most of what they want from it, little clash is likely; disruption will be caused only by a personality clash or by bad communications between the bargainers.

All bargainers must accept some deals which are at this disappointing level. But the bankruptcy courts are full of the records of people who were too nice to ask for what they wanted, too weak to argue their case, and too ready to accept a poor result too often.

Three things follow from this. The first principle is that you must know what you want before you start—it is no good waiting for the other party to make up your mind for you. He will set you up to expect what he wants you to expect from the deal. (It is your job to do this to him.)

If the contractor asks the customer what he wants to pay for the job, then the customer will give him a very low figure. The contractor must calculate what will be the cost of doing the full job properly, to the highest level of quality and workmanship and then suggest this to the customer. The customer will not run away in fright, although he can be expected to argue. He will need time to get used to the idea. But now he is seeing the contractor as an expert—not as a day laborer. The customer's expectations are changing.

The second principle is that once you know what you want, then you must hold out for it.

The builder should hold on to his full specification and fight for it. He should make the customer show him where he wants the quality to be cut, the work to be skimped, or the size of the total job to be reduced. If the customer works it out for himself, then he will convince himself of the need to have quality. The builder will reduce his total price, of course, but only after a struggle. But at least he will stay in business. He may even become rich. And it should be noted that the customer is more likely to get a good job done.

Bargainer's motto:

A good bargain is one which is good for both sides.

But you can be too strong. The construction world is full of contractors who made strong demands on weak sub-contractors, offering a huge volume of work but at knock-down rates which would require a very tightly controlled business to handle profitably. These little businesses are anything but tightly controlled. If they were efficient they would not be going for this kind of cut-price work in the first place. So, half-way through the contract, they start to cut the corners. They use sub-standard material, they skimp on the workmanship and the labor where it cannot be seen and detected. They scrape what living they can from the work, and then they go broke, leaving behind them a bad job and an angry contractor.

Question for hard bargainers:

If the other party goes bust,
could it have been your fault?

The contractor blames the sub-contractor, but in reality it was his own fault in the first place. He was too strong in his demands. He pressed them down too hard. He forgot one of the basic questions of bargaining: can the other side deliver his part of the bargain?

Mrs. Thatcher wanted a settlement near the £900 million level. The EEC countries wanted a settlement near the £300 million level. One party, or both, would have to alter their expectations if a deal were to be done. The first to break was Germany, with an offer of £350 million. This was rejected by Britain. Later, Germany began to talk of offering £800 million, but for one year only. This also was rejected, because Mrs. Thatcher argued for a continuing reduction over the years.

By February, two months after Dublin, Britain had accepted that there was going to be no quick deal. The British budget in April allowed for the full contribution to be paid to the EEC. After this, the advantage of time was now on Britain's side.

Shortly, the EEC countries would have to agree to an increase in the payments to farmers in the Community. Every member had to agree to this or the decision would not go through. France and Germany both wanted the payments increased for political reasons. Later in the year Presidential elections were due to be held in both countries. Neither government wanted to upset its own farming bloc. Mrs. Thatcher made no overt threat to withhold her agreement on this farming issue; she did not even link the issues together. But everyone knew that Britain would only come into line on agriculture payments if there were agreement on her Community budget payments. A meeting of EEC Foreign Ministers in May broke up without an agreement, and with the Germans withdrawing their suggestion of £800 million for one year.

But such a "withdrawal" is meaningless. Once an offer has been made, then the other party knows what they can achieve. It is almost impossible to withdraw it, unless the offer has been linked to some concession from the other party and is therefore conditional.

Bargainers should note:

Once you have made them an offer,
you have made them an offer.

Gradually, Mrs.Thatcher was moving the EEC members up towards her own level of expectations. She was proving several of the basic rules of bargaining. She set her sights on a high figure; she held firmly to this demand; and she refused to make the first major concession. Once the EEC members had made the first major move towards Britain's case, then they continued to move in the same direction.

The EEC countries finally settled on an agreement of around £800 million for two years, plus an undertaking to continue the same level of arrangement for year three, when the saving would be higher because of inflation.

Most bargaining situations are not crystallized so sharply as in the dispute between the EEC and Britain. In practice, one party usually has a clear idea of what he wants from the deal, while the other party is making up his mind. This represents an enormous opportunity for the bargainer who knows what he wants.

He has to arouse the interest of the other party, of course. He must explore the needs of the other party and the opportunities which lie available to him. But, right from the outset, he can signal the direction and the strength of his demands to the other party. More than this, he can initially go as high as he dares, up to and sometimes a little beyond his "best deal" limits. As the other party views the case presented to him, he starts to share the same perception of the deal as his opposite number. Once the bargainer has got him there, the task is to keep him there, and to stop him moving to any other idea, or any other level of expectation.

Star salesmen, for example, know how important it is to ask for the moon. In a developed economy, five people out of every hundred will be selling things for a living. The world devotes a gigantic proportion of its financial resources to recruiting, training, motivating, and managing sales specialists. Books are written by the thousands; courses are run; sales results are quantified, qualified, measured, assessed and reported upon in minute details.

All authorities agree that there can be an enormous difference in results obtained between a weak and unskilled sales specialist and a star performer, a real high flyer.

And yet no one has yet been able to measure accurately "star" qualities. Everyone would like to know what makes a "star" sales performer, but the plain fact is that star sales people are not cast in a common mold. Apart from generalities such as their high confidence and expert knowledge, on practically all other counts they are wildly different from each other. Some are introvert, some extrovert. Some have empathy and share the buyer's viewpoint. There is evidence that it helps if they are drawn from the buyer's industry, if they themselves have been a customer for what they sell. Some work very hard and are highly motivated. Some are lazy, and yet they still obtain results. Nearly every sales manager agrees that whatever the distinctive quality is, it must be inside the man. It is something which he brings himself to the job. Training will help everyone to do better, but you cannot train an ordinary person to be a star.

My own personal observation, uncluttered by scientific assessment, and backed by dedication to my own prejudices, is that there are three common characteristics of star sales performers.

One is that they are often difficult, and slightly rogue personalities to manage. The salesman who causes most trouble to management is often the star. He is the one who seldom reports on time, he complains more about management policy, he argues with decisions and often fails to carry out instructions. He is disruptive at sales conferences and hacks his way through company politics without realizing the sensitivities of the people concerned. If the sales force is in revolt, then the star is in there somewhere. Not leading it, perhaps, but stirring it up. In short, the star is unemployable. He will never make it to top management. There is only one reason why the company keeps him. It is because he outsells everyone else.

The second characteristic of the star is that he seldom remains a true star outside his chosen field of experience. If the star leaves the industry, or even if he leaves his company, then he is unlikely to be a star again. He will always be good, he will always be amongst the best, perhaps. But he will lose that diamond edge from his experience which made him a star originally.

But the principal factor which, for me, separates stars from ordinary sales mortals, is their devotion to big deals. They find it boring and time-wasting to handle little deals. New recruits to the world of selling insurance are often to be found clustered around the stars. This is because the stars frequently give away leads to new business. They pass around snippets of information, small prospects for the new insurance agents to land and thereby to earn their commission. The stars could get this business themselves and boost their own earnings. But they do not bother. They are interested only in the big deals. They will spot one hundred sales prospects, pick the top five and go only for them.

Stars do not take trial orders. Stars do not accept minor shares of the prospect's business. Not unless these are specific strategies they are using to get the whole of the business. They are interested in all or nothing.

What the star salesman seems to do is to implant in the other man's mind the idea that this is going to be a big and important deal. The benefits to the other party are substantial, but will only be realized if the deal is done on a big enough scale. This bargaining objective then determines the rest of the star's approach.

It determines who he deals with in the other company. (He seldom sees juniors or subordinates—always senior personnel with decision-making authority.) It determines how he presents himself and his case. (He shows them he is important—at least as important as they are.) It determines his "preselling." (They always know that he and his company are powerful and they look forward to meeting him.) And, more than anything else, he never lets them take their sights off the big deal. He will not allow them to drift down. If he accepts a small result, it is always because he has sold them the next stage of the bigger result already and he is getting them moving towards him.

He does two other things which are very important also. He always delivers more than people expect. He never lets them become disappointed with him, and he never oversells.

Many salesmen do oversell. They promise more than they can deliver. In this way they take a long walk off a short pier, because their reputation is destroyed subsequently.

BARGAINING TIME

The time-scale of the bargaining process affects bargaining objectives. At first, there is often a hazy definition of the outer limits of both parties' expectations. In time these become firmer. Delay can be used to strengthen one party's hand if time is on his side.

An investment banker, for example, might be quite excited at the prospect of putting a big deal together. He may have an appointment with the chairman of a company which he knows is in a little financial difficulty and which he thinks might be good for a take-over by one of his clients. So his expectations of success are high to start with; he will be thinking of a fairly low offer to start with.

But when he meets the chairman he finds a man full of confidence and vitality. The chairman shows the banker how well funded his company is, and displays his latest healthy business results. He also mentions that he has spurned another offer of a take-over.

This reaction from a man who is supposed to be grasping at the financial

---

BARGAINING TIME

Early sessions	Later sessions	Settlement

At the start each party will have wide expectations and will attempt to clarify its own aims and structure the aims of the other party.	Later, the margins begin to narrow, and the wilder possibilities are excluded.	Towards the end, the final settlement area becomes clearer.

---

lifeline held out by the banker is bad news. The banker now has to think of a much larger offer in order to entice the chairman. What the chairman has done is to lower the banker's expectations. The banker cannot achieve his top "desirable" result. He now has two broad options. He can continue with the dialogue, having been moved up towards the chairman's expectations. Or he can politely withdraw, leaving the door open for contact to be made later. The second option carries the risk that a rival offer might be made to the chairman (who could perhaps solicit such offers quietly to see what competitive bids he can get) and the deal might be lost. Alternatively, the chairman might be using a little bluff to talk up the bid. In this case, should the banker prepare to walk out, the chairman might hold the banker at the bargaining table by indicating that he is still willing to talk further. But this result can only come about if he sees that the banker is prepared to walk away, and if he believes that the banker means it. Time might not be on his side if he is in financial difficulties but he must not show this position.

By this kind of exchange, the original expectation levels are modified. No serious disruption is caused by deadlock at the start, provided that the door is left open to meet again. Of course, the competition may be let in, or the delay may alter the bargaining power of one side or the other. But the purpose of the initial meeting is to explore the situation, and for each party to feel its way towards a firmer idea of what deal might be possible in the end.

As time proceeds, then the detailed arguments often become sharper and harder. Play-acting, posturing, and signalling characterize the early moves, but gradually the aims of each party become clearer. Each party must move towards the other, but one party will generally move more than the other. This could be due simply to the skill of the people involved.

A deadlock at the later stages can be very serious. Very substantial emotional involvement is tied up with the aims and ambitions of each party; it is common and sensible for the leaders of each bargaining team to withdraw during the middle stages, while their subordinates agree on the details. The bosses can then be used to resolve major disputes and to tie up the final deal.

Stopping them from making up their minds in the wrong way is just as important to you as getting them to make up their minds your way. Signals can be used to show how important is the contentious issue; you can tell them, "We are now on the one issue which causes more breakdowns than any other." Asking them to hold off the question is another way: "Would you keep an open mind on that issue, if we were to review this other issue?" Reminding them of the value of collaboration rather than conflict is another way. "Can we reconstruct the deal so as to give you more of what you want as well as to give us more of what we want?" But the best way is to keep the issues fluid and open, to maintain a flexible attitude during the sessions. This is not to give anything away, but to prevent them from making up their minds against your sticking point.

SETTING UP THEIR EXPECTATIONS

You must float your ideas into their minds. You must also stop them from becoming committed to any wrong ideas. A wrong idea is any idea which does not suit you.

In setting up the deal that you want, you should make five factors work for you. You should carefully work out your opening moves, conveying signals to them of what you expect. You should be *conditioning* them, before and during the debate, to accept your view of the issue. You should *hold* to *your view*, taking care to emphasize the benefits of your case to them. You should use *delay*, and possibly even deadlock, early in the process if this will help to change their minds. And you should make your *opening demands* high, and not give way on them too easily.

To try to alter the other man's mind late in the bargaining process is extremely difficult. Mentally he is assured of realizing some of his hopes from the deal and he will react violently and often emotionally when he realizes that he may not gain his own way after all. A violent disruption of the relationship can be experienced over something quite small late in the discussions, even when major hurdles have been overcome satisfactorily during the earlier stages.

So if you must press down their expectations, then be sure to do so early in the debate, if your bargaining power is strong. If your power is weak, then you may be forced to leave such difficult issues towards the end because you want to maintain their interest in your proposition. The sooner you can start them seeing things your way, the better.

In Jakarta, one government purchasing officer has been taking the arms and legs off his suppliers for years. Here is a typical example of how he operates. The construction of a new power station in the island of Java was open to tender. Part of the contract required a very large generator to be purchased. Only half a dozen companies in the world could supply such a size and the manufacturers operated through local agents in Indonesia.

The agent representing the leading German manufacturer was surprised not to be included upon the tender list. The purchasing officer refused to see him. After the bids had been received from the competitors in the United States, Japan, Britain and France, the purchasing officer called in the agent. He vowed the agent to secrecy. Then he showed him the competitors' quotations, adding that if the agent could come up with a price reduction of 10% on the lowest, then he would probably get the order.

In this way, he started to structure the agent's expectations.

Notice that the purchasing officer did not invite him on to the tender list in the first place. At that stage, the German company would have tendered a high price based upon a "full cost" basis, recovering all their allocated overhead and profit. Once committed to this price it would have been difficult to move them. Instead, the purchasing officer led them to think they would not get the chance at all.

The agent was now excited at the prospect of landing the valuable contract and he now had a specific target to take to his principal in Germany. The German company grumbled and had difficulty making up its mind. The agent chipped in a little bit of his own margin to help to get the price down. He finally submitted his quotation of about 10% lower than the lowest of the others.

Then the purchasing officer squeezed the agent some more. He simply did nothing. He would not take telephone calls from the agent, he would not see him. The agent's spirits dropped again, he felt he had lost the contract. Finally he got an interview. The purchasing officer apologized for the delay and explained that according to government policy he must obtain one more quotation and this had just arrived. Unfortunately, this new quotation was 2½% below the German price. This time, the agent could have the contract subject to government ratification if he could reduce his quotation by about 3%. The agent flew to Germany. There was a world recession in the market for capital equipment; most governments and public authorities were deferring expenditure where they could. The Germans agreed to lower the price by 3%. The agent took back this new quotation. The company was now selling well below full cost.

The purchasing officer was very pleased. He congratulated the agent. He said that the next day they would discuss terms. "What terms?" asked the agent. "The usual stage payments will apply." The purchasing officer countered by saying the company would have to meet the terms of its rivals in these days of high inflation and interest rates, etc.

After a great deal of argument, and with the help of a loan from the German government, the manufacturer agreed to meet the competitor's terms, which allowed a full eighteen months credit—an enormous concession.

The purchasing officer had now pushed the agent and the company to the limit—or very nearly. He had just one more card to play. A small ace.

He visited the German manufacturer in Cologne and saw the managing director to finalize the deal. He asked if the company had found the offer of long-term credit expensive to finance. Eager to show how generous they had been, the German executives calculated the actual cost of the interest they were providing. The purchasing officer pulled out the contract from his brief case, already signed by his senior ministers. He explained that with the large oil revenues flowing into Indonesia, the government had no need for the long-term credit at that time, so if the company just took the cash cost of the credit off the quotation as an extra discount, then he would be willing to pass over the contract. Otherwise, he was afraid that the Japanese..., etc.

In the end he did not get all of the final cash discount he asked for. But he did get half of it.

Tip for bargainers:

> Be careful of the man who
> swears you to secrecy.

He had succeeded by using his power to the full and by forcing down the expectations of the agent and of the German manufacturer. Bit by bit he made them come to him, once he had got them moving then he kept them moving. This purchasing officer is always strong. He is one of the few there who cannot be bought or bribed, and he will not allow suppliers to deal behind his back or with his superiors. Any sign of that automatically cuts them off from the next tender.

To position the other party to see your point of view and to adopt your own perspective of the deal requires a series of signaling moves. The first signals start before the debate begins.

MAKE THEM SEE ONLY YOUR CASE

The next most important thing is the way the debate is conducted. In any deal, each party approaches the issue with his own particular "tunnel vision." Each party sees mostly his own case. Each has his own value system, his own expectations and his own pressures. Each has different hopes for the outcome of the deal. To alter the expectations of the other party, you must make them look down your particular tunnel most of the time; you must make them see things your way, value the things you value, hope for the same outcome for which you hope. You must present them with the ideal proposition to suit their requirements—and that is your case. You may be arguing the case in terms of the benefits to them, but it is always your proposal you are debating. Ignore the way they calculate the benefits to you of their own case. That leads towards your weakness.

Bargainers should note:

> *In any debate there is only one correct*
> *point of view—and that's yours.*

Insurance salesmen, for example, are often terrified of one particular objection they meet frequently from prospects. When the prospect tells them that he does not believe in life insurance as a means of saving money because the effect of inflation will wash away the value of his savings, then many insurance salesmen collapse. They have been thoroughly conditioned by their prospects to see things this way. They argue unconvincingly for their own case from then on. In reality their own ideas have been turned away from their own case and into the direction of the prospect's case.

But one star life insurance salesman for a small company welcomes this objection. In fact, he insists on raising it himself if the prospect is not going to. He actually manages to close deals on this question. He looks at the issue of inflation down a different tunnel; he sees it as an enormous opportunity, not as a threat.

When his prospect raises the issue of inflation he calmly tells him that inflation is a great help, to him, the prospect. "How is that?" asks the prospect. "Because it makes it easier for you to pay the premium each year."

The salesman has noted that salaries and wages go up in line with inflation. He makes his prospects see that if they pay $1,000 this year, then it will be easier to find the same sum next year. All they have to do to maintain the real value of their savings is to top up their payments as they can afford it out of their increased earnings.

He lands three times as many life contracts as any other salesman in the company. He always invites the prospects to play his game, and to look down his tunnel. Then they see things differently.

THE USE OF DELAY

Delay will also alter a person's expectations. A personnel manager was hiring a chief engineer. One man came to the interview lacking the qualifications of another candidate but with several excellent personal qualities of his own. The personnel man told him on the spot that he had not got the chief engineer's job and explained the reasons when asked. He offered the man a job as works engineer in the company's principal factory. This was a good job and would suit the man very well, paying much the same money as the chief engineer was to be paid. The man was angry at being turned down for the job he came for, and stormed off after an emotional and upsetting scene.

Later in the year much the same situation occurred with the hiring of a factory personnel manager. This time the woman who was not suited for the job was not told immediately. They gave her three weeks or so to get used to the idea that she was not going to be offered the job. Then they asked her to come back and see them, not about the original job but about an alternative vacancy that they thought would suit her talents particularly well. She did come to see them, and they hired themselves a very good company administration manager.

Tip for bargainers:

> *If you are going to let them down,*
> *let them down lightly.*

What they had done was to let her down gradually through using delay. Delay will wear down the stoutest heart in the end. If the other party has high hopes, which you cannot fulfill, then let the matter drift, and drift. They will bring themselves down, and you will get what you want.

THE OPENING STANCE

The most potent signal of all is the level of the first offer. The opening demands made by each party on the other begin to firm up the anticipations of both parties. The first demand sets the outside limit on the deal. And the first answering demand sets the opposite outside limit. In negotiations terminology, this represents the opposing stances of the two parties.

Should you make the first demand or should you let him make the first demand? The advantage to the man opening the bidding is that he can press for his upper limit. Once this is on the table, then it becomes difficult for the other party to move too far away from it without losing contact. But the danger of making the opening demand is that it may not be high enough, in which case a great deal has been lost. Alternatively, it may be so ridiculously high that it is out of reach of the other party.

Consider the opening stance as being principally a test of the other party. Where the bargainer is fairly certain that the other party is not too sure of his ground—he might not be used to this kind of contract, for example, and has little idea of what it will cost—then it will pay the bargainer to make the opening demand, on the high side. Ideally, it should be higher than the "best deal" limit but floated in such a way that it does not become a formal request. To talk constantly about a similar large contract for a different company, for example, and to use this constantly as a third-party illustration is a good way; or to float a hypothetical situation, "just to see where it takes us," is another way. If the other party demures strongly, then the bargainer can drop the demand down a little without losing his credibility. If the other party continues the conversation concentrated around the high demand, then that is a good sign.

Where the bargainer is sure that the other party knows exactly what he is doing, then he should still float large ideas, but he should let the other party come to him first with an offer.

His immediate reaction at that moment is very important. He should either express some form of "shock-horror," or he should pretend that he has not heard and ignore the issue. What he should not do is to respond immediately with a counter demand, unless this is part of a planned maneuver. If he does, then the game will become competitive and the bargainer will be pressed into showing his hand. The best reaction is to say nothing and think hard. This puts the other party under immediate pressure; the more silent the bargainer, the more the other party will gradually lower his sights. The bargainer can then see how genuine is the other party's demand, and how much it is simply a fake.

TACTICS AND PLAYS

Kite flying.

Kite flying gambits are carried on at all stages of the bargaining process. They can be used to warn the other party of dangers ahead, to set up their expectations, to try out possible solutions, to get them used to difficult ideas. Signals are designed to creep into the other party's mind and to nag away there.

"The man across the street was very disappointed that he let his house go at this price," says Mr. Sells, "because he found he could have got $4,000 more a few weeks later."

"I am having a whole lot of trouble over selling my own house. I think we may have to take $6,000 less," replies Mr. Purchase. "The market for selling houses is very bad these days, isn't it?"

The counter to this technique is to do nothing. Signals call for no action on your part, so don't act and don't provide any response signals by your behavior.

Baiting the hook

Fishermen often cast little bits of bait around the area of their hook, to get the fish nibbling. If the fish nibbles at the main bait the fishermen might not strike immediately. They have the patience to wait until the fish is firmly hooked. They strike then, and not before. The same is true of bargainers.

"Your little girl likes riding, does she?" says Mr. Sells. "Where do you keep your pony now? What a pity the deal does not include our meadow on the other side of the stream."

"Does that belong to you as well?" asks Mr. Purchase. "Let's deal with the house issue first and we'll worry about the meadow later," replies Mr. Sells.

The counter is to ignore the bait at first but remember it. When the going gets tough later, then it can be included in the settlement package. Keep your mind on your main objective.

We always play our rules

Here is another fateful gambit if you allow them to use it. Never, ever, work to their order forms, their procedures, their practices. Never sign their terms of business. Always make them sign your terms of business.

"Why don't we have my attorney draw up the contract? That will save you the legal costs." It will also make a fortune for him as well.

And you want to get the rules established *before* you start. Looking at the rule book after the game is over is no good.

Tell me, how do the other teams play?

This is a devilish play, which is often nasty, and is often effective. The intention is to get the other party to reveal all that they know about their own opposition. They compete to give the dirt on their rivals. This way, an uninformed buyer becomes well informed, because he knows of the weaknesses of everyone. As they put their benefits to him, he puts their weaknesses to them. He is in a better position to evaluate all the deals and to select the best one.

Mr. Sells wants a real estate agent to handle his house sale. He sees four of them, taking care to let each one know that the choice of agent lies between Mr. Agent and his major competitor. Mr. Agent advocates an exclusive arrangement with one agent (himself). Mr. Sells suggests that he does not like the other man much, the major competitor, and could Mr. Agent tell him, in confidence of course, whether the other man's reputation is of the highest? Most people will abuse their rivals if they can. They are uncomfortable while they do it, but they do it just the same if invited.

You will lose the replay

With this technique they make the future look bleak for you. You could be in a lot of trouble if you do not do the deal they want now.

"You are lucky having me here." says Mr. Purchase. "Mortgages are hard to get and the position is getting worse. The whole market is drying up. If you don't sell now, then you could be in trouble. It's lucky I've got the cash."

All out attack

In bargaining if you don't ask you won't get. If you ask for the lot, you won't always get it, but you will sometimes. If you ask for a little you will never get the lot. One big attack often carries all before it.

"I know we have been talking about the house, but quite honestly I wonder if you would consider the whole lot, the carpets and furniture and furnishings, the garden furniture, and including your meadow over the stream. Do you make much use of the camper, because we'd be quite interested in that as well. How about an overall package? Then you can make a clean start yourself in your new house."

The counter? If they want the bits badly they can buy them. Bit by bit. No package.

SUMMARY

The quality of the deal which is finally done is usually determined by the way the deal has been set up in the first place. It is important for the bargainer to identify the limit of the best possible deal he can do—this is just below the level of his opening demand or offer. He should aim high, and he should signal his expectations to the other party. If this can be done before the two parties get together then this may be helpful. The bargainer should also set a lower limit; his "worst" deal. This is the point at which he would prefer to do no deal. He will work very hard indeed to avoid being dragged this far.

If the two parties are well apart in their initial expectations, then deadlock may result. This is not necessarily a bad thing, although there is a danger that the strong party may then go ahead with a deal with a competitor. But it may be necessary to cause deadlock in order to change the other party's mind. If the personal warmth can be maintained in the relationship then it should not be too difficult for the two parties to get together later.

Stalling and delay may be useful tactics to persuade the other party to modify their expectations. But a radical change of mind is an emotional issue, and great care must be taken that the personal relationship between the two parties is not ruptured. It is dangerous to trample upon the other party's hopes and emotions.

*   *   *

Now go back to the start of the chapter and complete the questionnaire again.

Probing and Presenting | 7

LEARNING MODULE

This short learning module is designed to teach the essentials of exploratory discussion before the chapter is read.

In some paragraphs, certain words appear in caps. These words are very important and are left out of succeeding paragraphs (represented by a dotted line). Please fill in the correct word. You can check the correct response each time at the end of the book. This is not a test: it is a self-development exercise.

*   *   *

Early in the discussion it is necessary to explore the position of the other party by the means of an OPEN *question. This allows the other party to speak freely and to reveal his attitudes.*

Q.1   *The most common words, well-known to trained journalists are: What, Where, When, How, and Why—these are most frequently found at the start of............... questions. The other party generally elaborates with further information.*

Correct Response: OPEN

(The rest of the responses are contained at the end of the book.)

Q.2   *It is important to listen carefully to the answers to............... questions and to interpret the answers within the other party's frame of reference. Listen also for the feeling behind the answers as well as the meaning. This indicates their emotional reaction to the issue.*

Q.3   *It is important to hear out the other party fully. In our eagerness to make our own points we can sometimes latch on to something the other party says which helps us to make our case. It is a mistake to interrupt when the purpose is to explore information............... questions may need to be followed by further............... questions; sometimes at quite late stages in the discussion.*

Q.4   *When we wish to move towards shaping the other party's responses towards our case then we can use a* LEADING *question. This obtains very specific responses, which are then used to help our presentation. The answers to these questions are often likely to be short, whereas a more discursive answer is likely to be obtained from . . . . questions.*

Q.5   *The words —Do you, Did you, Could you, Would you, Have you, Are you — these are often used at the start of . . . . questions. Such questions should not be asked so obviously that the other party can easily see the intention behind them; neither should they be asked too often. Their intention is to lead the other party in the direction we want them to go.*

Q.6   *Generally such questions are asked after the background information has been obtained through . . . . questions and the line of approach becomes obvious. But it is possible to ask too many questions and to make the other party suspicious. It is usually wise to exchange some information mutually, but taking care to reveal only what we plan to reveal. It is important to listen for the general theme revealed by the other party and to ignore incidental comments. Generally the specific answers obtained through . . . . questions are the ones we want to hear.*

Q.7   *When listening for the general information obtained from . . . . questions, it may be important to sense what is not being said. This gap may need to be probed. When we obtain the specific answers we want from asking a . . . . question, we should supply positive support.*

Q.8   *A further kind of question seeks to obtain confirmation or agreement on a point. This is a* CONFIRMATION *question, one of the most commonly used in discussion and it obtains the simple answer, either "Yes" or "No." It is the simplest kind of . . . . question but one which is often very badly used.*

Q.9   *Most commercial discussions are based upon cooperative goodwill between the parties. When one party gives the answer "no" there is temporarily a break in the relationship. Often the reason is because the . . . . question was asked in the wrong way.*

Q.10   *For example, a department store salesgirl may ask the customer, "Can I help you?" This is the wrong way of approach (although most of them do it just like this). The reason is because the customer may reply, "No, thanks, I'm just looking," whereupon the salesgirl loses control over the situation and there is at least a temporary separation between the two parties. It may even be*

slightly difficult to bring them together again. All because she asked them
a . . . . question in the wrong way.

Q.11   *The right way for her to ask such a . . . . question is to say:*
"Would you like me to leave you to look around for a few moments longer,
madam?" If the answer is "Yes," then a feeling of goodwill is established. In
fact, the customer will not answer "No" at all. If she wants service she will
say so, and the salesgirl has achieved her objective. Conditioning the other
party to say "yes" throughout the discussion may be important.

Q.12   *With this kind of . . . . question and with the specific answers*
obtained from other kinds of . . . . questions, it is important that
we know what kind of answers we want, and we know what to do with them
when we have them. However, we may need to alter the other party's view
in a more direct way. For this we can use a slightly more aggressive WEAK-
ENING *question.*

Q.13   *This is designed to show our resistance to something the other party is saying.*
Such a . . . . question is designed to show up some flaw or illog-
icality in their case, and to put a little pressure on them. "How can you be
certain?" "Will you guarantee it?" "Does that square with what you said
earlier?" "Are you certain?" are typical examples.

Q.14   *Used persistently, it can change their expectations and cause them to alter*
their position or reduce their demands. But pressure tactics through the over-
use of . . . . questions must recognize the danger of creating an
argument and a socially hostile environment.

Q.15   *This technique can be fairly punishing to the other party. The use*
of . . . . questions should be limited to the times when one's bar-
gaining power needs to be reinforced. Such questions invite a counterattack
if they are presented in an aggressive manner. But very damaging questions
can be put quietly and easily at the right moment and the represents a more
effective attack.

Q.16   *If the other party is emotional, if they feel strongly on the issue, then*
such . . . . questions should be used with extreme care, if at all.
It may be more useful to provide positive reinforcement for those remarks they
make which are favorable to our case. This is called providing a SUPPOR-
TIVE *statement.*

Q.17   *Once the discussion is held on the merits of the case, then the other party*
should be encouraged when their views help our case by our
. . . . statement. "Yes, that's true," "That is very helpful," "I'm

sure you are right" are examples. When they say things which do not help us, then they should be ignored.

Q.18 *The other party should be made to see his position in a way that benefits us. That means we must recognize his position first and then by us-ing . . . . statements and behavior such as smiling and head nodding we will bring him our way. Negative techniques such as silence or unsmiling reactions or the more aggressive . . . . questions can be used to alter his position.*

Q.19 *In this way, through negative and positive actions, the other party's responses are shaped. But the need to have adequate information about the other party's pressures exists throughout the whole discussion. Sometimes the other party can be surprised into revealing his position through the use of sudden pressure such as a . . . . question being introduced in the midst of generally . . . . statements.*

Q.20 *It is useful if our . . . . statement is immediately led on to one of the BENEFITS of our case. This in an explanation of the advantages, which will accrue to the other party, and usually relates to some feature of our proposition. "Yes, that is a good point, and by doing it your way, we will complete the deal earlier."*

Q.21 *The other party is only interested in the features of our proposition in so far as they relate to specific . . . . which he will enjoy. If a machine tool salesman suggests using high quality steel, for example, this only becomes a benefit when it is translated into longer life or durability, or greater reliability for his customer.*

Q.22 *But the other party will have to be reassured of the . . . . to him and we do this by providing him with PROOF statements. If we say, "Our machines are the best," he thinks to himself that everyone can claim the same thing. But if we go on to show him an independent test report produced by an engineering laboratory of world stature, then he will believe us.*

Q.23 *Such a . . . . statement might relate to a distinctive feature of our proposition; or it might relate to some research or test evidence; or a third party example. A . . . . is unlikely to be taken on trust by the other party unless it is supported in some way by evidence.*

Q.24 *In most propositions there are several . . . . for the other party. We should start with the general . . . . and move then to specific ones. Each . . . . which is put across may need to be supported by a . . . . statement if it is questioned.*

Q.25 *But offer.............sparingly. Give him those that suit his needs, but keep as many as possible in reserve. These will be needed later to counter his resistance or to awaken his interest again, or to settle the deal.*

Probing and Presenting | 7

A certain company was saved from bankruptcy entirely by one man's distinctive questioning style. No proposals were made, no demands, no summaries of the situation. Yet one party in the dispute was caused to collapse completely, and a deal was done. All because one man asked questions, relentlessly.

What worried the company chairman was that if the little engineering company in his group went broke, then it might bring down his personal empire. He might himself be recalled to his head office in Johannesburg, and be given some non-job to keep him quiet until he could collect an early retirement pension.

And there was his wife to consider as well. She had made it very plain that she would not return to South Africa, she was happy only with her cluster of friends among the other expatriates in the African capital where they were living.

Of such pressures are bargainers made.

For himself, the chairman would not directly interfere in the dispute; it had never been his style to interfere with operations. On the other hand, after three years of intercompany warfare, he could knock his two chief executives' silly heads together.

The background was quite simple. One company, a little engineering plant manufacturing and assembling agricultural equipment, was being raped by its brother company, the distributor of its products. Both were subsidiaries of the same group.

The distributor was vigorous and powerful in the market. Headed by a burly South African, it had a strong sales force, offered farmers an excellent service back-up and one-half of its sales came from products made by companies outside its parent group. The other half came from the troubled engineering company.

The engineering company was set up originally to service the requirements of the distributor alone. Whatever the distributor wanted, it made. The distributor set the quantities, and forced the prices down low. The distributor treated it as any other supplier, rejected poor quality, pressed the company hard for exceptional service. The products made could not be bought from elsewhere; they were suited only to the conditions of the market served by the distributor. The European engineer who ran the concern had tried to develop other export markets for its products, but was forced to accept that practically all its revenue came from the distributor. His company was making large losses which were getting larger.

What we have here is a typical conflict bargaining situation. Both parties are locked-in together and cannot escape from each other. It is exacerbated by the fact that one party is much stronger than the other—and it is not helped either by the fact that the two top men do not like each other. The chairman, who could sort out the problems with simple directives to each man, refuses to take part.

When two parties do not know each other, then they dance around each other carefully at first. They use probing techniques to question each other and they then try to drive each other down the tracks they want to follow.

When the two parties know each other very well, however, there is a tendency to make straightforward assumptions about the position of the other party. Long and well-established business relationships are usually characterized by a routine based upon experience.

The use of probing and leading questions in situations which are thoroughly familiar to us, where we know all the answers already is just as vital as when the two parties do not know each other.

Tip for bargainers:

Don't take the other party for granted.
Take them out to lunch.

The distributor stood upon his rights. "You get all my business in these products. We deserve special treatment. If it were not for us, you would be out of business. It is up to you to give us what we want. You must work efficiently to make the best profit you can," was his attitude towards the engineer.

The engineer was in a hopelessly weak position. Everyone knew his business was unprofitable; he had been dominated by the distributor for years. If he tried to exert pressure then the distributor simply increased his demands or made more complaints or rejected more goods. So he was lost.

The chairman called in a friend from outside the company, paid him a fee, and asked him to resolve the issue. The parent board in Johannesburg had complained about the quarterly returns and wanted the chairman to report to a meeting with them.

This consultant believed in making certain that other people came along with his views willingly. He wanted them to develop those views for themselves, if possible, because he found that people are more committed to conclusions which they arrive at, than to conclusions that are handed to them.

So the consultant rarely made statements. He asked questions; and continued asking questions, getting people to develop the answers for themselves. He made others propose solutions. If they wanted to find out his point of view and ask him a question then he would usually counter it with another question back to them. "What do you think, yourself?" they might ask him. "Well, how would you feel about such and such as an alternative?" he would reply. They would see the way his mind was working, but they themselves would be involved in providing the solution.

The consultant questioned the information on both sides. He made some private calculations about the overhead cost of maintaining the engineer's special services to the distributor, including new product development. He also made a surprising discovery. From the distributor, he found that the engineer's products accounted for half of the total sales value, but they earned 75% of the distributor's profit contribution. Furthermore, the products made by the engineer were those which had enabled the distributor to penetrate the farming market so easily and to defeat his competitors. Actually, he suspected that the distributor was not so efficient after all. The distributor would be out of business if it were not for the engineer.

This information was absolutely vital to the solution of the dispute. It had been available all along to the engineer if he had asked. He never thought to ask. Because of this, the company had lost thousands and was facing bankruptcy.

He asked his questions gently, but he also observed that the distributor's answers were very offhand and disinterested. He would have liked to ignore the consultant if he could. The consultant concluded that the distributor was not open to reason on the issue.

The bargaining was nearly over now—before the formal debate had begun. The consultant had followed the correct procedure. He had probed the case openly; he had asked both chief executives if they would consider certain alternatives. It was clear that the engineer would move but that the distributor would not. By asking people further down the line he realized that the distributor saw the issue as a trial of strength, and he had secured the support of his staff behind him. So the consultant made his move.

Four weeks later the chairman received a directive from his head office instructing him to shut down the engineering company within six weeks. He called for a plan for this from the engineer, who despondently agreed. He said nothing to the distributor, apart from noting the decision at a Board meeting.

Within five days the distributor was desperate. He knew perfectly well how important the engineer's products were to his business. He could get them from nowhere else because foreign exchange regulations made it impossible for him to import them in finished form. The chairman distanced himself from the distributor by going on holiday. The consultant could not be traced. The distributor was forced to go to the engineer and ask for his help.

Within three weeks a new proposal was on the chairman's table. The engineer would streamline the product range with the full agreement of the distributor. Some products would be trimmed in quality, others would bear substantial price increases. The cost of product development would be borne by the distributor and the engineer equally. Johannesburg withdrew its instruction to close down the engineering plant—indeed, top management had been puzzled at the request for such a memo in the first place.

The problems rumbled on for some time; but the arguments never had the same quality of desperation again.

Tip for bargainers:

Don't believe every memo they show you.

In order to motivate the other party towards our case, we must ourselves test the situation. We must find out their needs and wants; we must test out various plans or strategies and observe the reaction. When their reaction is favorable, we must note it and support it. Gradually we can drop the alternatives in order to concentrate upon the part of our case which is obtaining the right feedback.

This way, by understanding them and their needs, we can alter the shape of our proposition to suit them, or we can take more aggressive steps to alter their attitudes.

Information is power. The more we find out about them, then the more our bargaining power builds. Equally the reverse is true, they can weaken us by their probing. The rule is: get them to give you their information, but don't reveal your information to them.

In large and complex negotiations, it can be very useful to have informal discussions between the parties, but everyone should be on their guard. The object must be to gain information, and not to give it away.

In listening to the other party you should look beyond the actual words and to the general theme. Identify both the meaning of what they say and the feeling with which they say it. Ask yourself "Why?" do they say that. You are looking for what a salesman would call a buying signal. Such signals can be very light and delicate—perhaps just an expression of heightened interest at one moment, a change in posture, a support for your point of view.

Take particular notice if they flatter you, or if they go out of their way to antagonize you or to threaten or shock you. Treat such actions as being independent of you yourself. They are manipulative techniques; you should ask yourself "Why are they doing this?"

Bargainers should note:

> *When they praise you it does not mean you are great.*
> *It means they want something from you.*

THE PRESENTATION OF THE CASE

In most bargaining situations of any complexity, one party will be expected to make a presentation to the other. The other party can be expected to test the case which is presented.

If you have to make a presentation to the other party, whatever else you do, don't prepare a long monologue with detailed arguments to deliver to them. You will have lost their attention within 30 seconds.

You must never do this because: you are giving away too much information; they cannot absorb all your material in their minds; you are not shaping the material to their needs; you are not allowing them to give you a reaction; you cannot be sure you are carrying their agreement; you are offering your case as a hostage to fortune. In short, they will not understand it. They will not agree with it. They will think that you are inept and self-centered.

Bargainers should take heed:

If you want your competitors to get the business,
then do all the talking, all the time.

The first principle for the presenter is to create a climate of confidence. The other party needs to be reassured, all the time. They want to know they are dealing with someone who is straight, and whose word can be relied upon. It is vital to be absolutely reliable, to turn up on time to meetings, to do things you say you are going to do, and to do them on time. Reliability does not mean perfection—everyone makes mistakes, but the confident man admits the mistakes. The owner of a very successful company making kitchen units tells his customers that he himself makes more mistakes than anyone else in the factory. He goes on to explain that this is because he makes more decisions than anyone else. But the points are not lost on the customer—first, the man is a decision-maker; second, the man is confident enough to admit making some mistakes; third, by the sound of it his people do not make many mistakes (because the owner can be seen to be personally a very efficient man). It is by such techniques as this that reassurance is provided to the other party.

Shape the presentation towards the needs of the other party. If you are certain that they will react unfavorably to a part of your case then anticipate this by building your answers to their questions in your presentation.

If you let them raise a major objection, or try to slip past a weakness in your case in the hope they will not notice it, then this will destroy your posture. You will then be forced to answer their objections with what will sound like weak excuses. If a part of your case is weak, while the rest of it is strong, then admit the weakness yourself, but ensure that the sum of all the other benefits you offer will outweigh the weakness.

Don't lie. Lies will destroy you in the end. Lies seep into your personality, they undermine your confidence, they sap your morale. Lying is the strategy of the weak man. Be an advocate, by all means. You are expected to use the arguments which suit your case, to be selective. But don't lie. That is a stupid thing to do.

Maintain your integrity. The owner of the kitchen unit factory developed his technique originally when he found that a good way of getting on with his own boss, when he was a lad, was to go along and confess to some error, some small mistake. He found that bosses were never angry with him. He found that they were actually reassured because here was a youngster who had the courage to confess, who knew when he had made an error, and who could be relied upon. If, during a crisis, a mistake had been made and if he said he was not responsible, then they believed him absolutely. The boy developed this early technique into a major weapon he could use in later business life.

Note for bargainers:

A little confession can be very good for the soul,
because it reveals your undoubted honesty.

If a presentation is to be long and complicated then cut it into small chunks, separated in time. Supply visual evidence of the points you must make, and supply proofs of any claims you make.

Remember that people can only absorb about three to five facts at a time, so keep the facts few in number, reinforce them, and say them in different ways. Make sure that each section of your presentation is linked to a benefit for the other party.

Bargainers should remember the rules for public speakers:

> *Tell 'em what you are going to tell 'em;*
> *tell 'em; then tell 'em what you have*
> *just told them.*

Make certain that the main benefit is shown to relate to a problem of theirs. Remember your object is to influence their behavior, and in a way which favors you. To do this they must have the right attitude to you and to your case. In order to develop the right attitude they must be able to identify the problem they are trying to solve.

Always dig into the problem. Use questions to see that they understand what you are saying. Use questions to secure their agreement and to make sure they are coming with you. If they are not with you, go back to the problem. If you hammer the problem, then they will often see the solution for themselves, and it will be the solution *you* wanted them to see in the first place. On your presentations, make them do the work—not you.

Have you ever thought of being in business for yourself? Perhaps you could be a consultant in your line of business. To become a modest-sized consultancy you have to become known for your expertise. You have to mix among client companies, make contacts at the top, and sooner or later you will be asked to submit a proposal for solving some company's problem.

So you will take a look at the client's business. You will spot what is wrong and what is needed for you to put it right. You will put forward to him a proposal for the engagement of your services which outlines what you expect to do, how long it will take and what will be the expense. In this way you will build a little business, lead a varied life, and land probably half of the assignments where you have submitted proposals.

Why run a little business when you could run a big business? Why land half of them, when you could land most of them? Instead of being poor and happy, why not be rich and happy? Be like Arthur D. Little or the other top consultancies—like a little. Use the nodding technique.

To reach these heights you will have to alter your proposals. Concentrate really hard on the first few pages. Write them out several times over. Make them interesting, readable, challenging. These pages go under the heading called "Statement of the Problem."

When you do your preliminary survey of the company, keep asking the people who work there what they think the problems are. Ask at all levels. Get all the views. There will be a common consistency about these analyses. Then what you must do is to rewrite the problems in your own way, using your own distinctive perspectives. It is their overall problem examined by your attitude. If you do this properly, you will not have to bother too much with what you propose to do as the solution.

Once your proposal has got the client nodding his head in agreement in the first few pages, considering you a genius to be able to dissect their condition so quickly and with such refreshing originality, they will be prepared to buy almost any solution you put forward. They will nod all the way through your costs as well.

So those of you who are used to submitting formal "quotations" to customers which simply state all the specifications of your submission and your costs should go back to your companies immediately, have the existing quotation procedures scrapped and replaced by a proposal which mostly concerns the client and his problem—and less of you and your solutions.

Make the presentation of your case effective and memorable. If you can select one simple highlight and demonstrate it in a memorable fashion, then this may be sufficient for the whole task.

A British company making a filter kit for home winemaking enthusiasts took an exhibition stand at a convention of home winemakers in San Francisco. Interest was low, and the executive was despondent. The whole thing needed a spark.

A woman came to the stand and told the executive that the kit did not look strong enough. He teased her, challenged her to bring all her friends back in half an hour and he would prove how strong it was. The crowd gathered, including a local television reporter who had come to the exhibition to see if there was any news in it.

The executive picked up his product and threw it hard against a wall. He invited others to do the same. Everybody had fun and the story made local television news. He was congratulated afterwards by the organizers of the convention for getting them on television. He did not do a lot of business. But he did gain a lot of attention.

Tip for bargainers:

> If a picture is worth a thousand words,
> then a demonstration is worth a million.

SECURITY

Many bargainers will be involved in long and difficult studies with the other party. This may involve many consultations between experts. Be very careful about security among members of your own team. The cost of one ham sandwich and half a glass of beer to this supplier was the entire net profit on a contract worth $2 million.

A machine tool manufacturer was bidding for the United States contract in competition with suppliers from Germany and the USA. The Board of the customer company had agreed to accept their bid but the purchasing officer

told the president that he intended getting the price down first, from the supplier.

He first called up the salesman, saying "I'm sorry to let you down in this
way, Joe,..."

Joe immediately sensed that he was not going to get the order and asked if
this were so. The purchasing officer said: "Well, you know if it had been my
decision, you could have had the order tomorrow, but the Board has taken it
out of my hands. Just for the sake of 2½%", I think it's crazy...."

Joe was astonished to hear that he had lost by only 2½%. He asked if there
were an opportunity of keeping the deal open for a day. The purchasing officer
told him that he should really have signed the letter to the rival supplier, but
he would keep the deal on ice for 24 hours. "But I can't open up the question
with the Board for just 2⅓%," he said. "You'll have to do better than that."
That is always a killer phrase, when used by a buyer on a salesman.

The salesman asked his manager, who asked his director, who was panicked
by the loss of an order he was banking on. Business was very slack. Sales were
well below budget.

The director said, "All right, you can go up to 3½%, but call me first if you
have to go higher. And whatever you do, get the order. I'll patch it up with
the old man later."

So the purchasing officer was offered 3½% and accepted gratefully. The sales
engineer thought that 3½% was nothing really, because it represented only
$70,000 out of a $2 million sale. The manager realized that the discount would
have to be paid for actually out of the gross profit on the deal, which would
total about $600,000 after the cost of materials and sub-contract had been taken
into account, so the effect of the discount would be bigger than the salesman
thought.

But actually, the discount wiped out most of the net profit on the deal. This
was calculated originally at around $60,000. Since the company had got the
business in the first place, then they need not have given the extra discount. So
why did it happen? (Apart from the fact that the salesman was a bad bargainer,
and the purchasing officer was a good one.)

It happened because six weeks beforehand the salesman had met the customer's chief engineer to discuss technical points. He had explained that his company's sales were not going well and that his company was under pressure. It
was no more than a casual conversation. Later, the chief engineer had a similar
casual conversation with his own purchasing officer. He told him what the
salesman had said.

That was all the information that the buyer needed. He now knew the
company would be soft on price and could be squeezed.

Tip for managers of bargainers:

Somewhere, this very minute,
one of your staff is being conned
by the other party.

When several people are involved in the presentation of information, it is vital to rehearse them. It is vital to make sure that all substantive communications are fed to the other party only through the team leader. And it is vital to make sure that security is very tight amongst the rest of the team wherever they cannot be supervised.

It is the other party's task to worm the information out of your team. And they will do it, and use it effectively against you, if you do not take steps to avoid it.

But you can do this to them, of course. Their security is their problem. Not yours.

PRESENTING THE DIFFICULT CASE

When presenting substantial demands, you must give the other party time to become accustomed to them. It may pay for you to arrange two meetings. Signal your intentions at the first meeting, let them get used to the idea, and then move in with your full demand later.

People need time to become accustomed to a major change. They will also need reassurance. When you are to present a radical move, do not spell out the details at first. The first objective is to get them unsettled with the existing arrangement and to indicate to them that a big proposal is going to come forward. You might try a fishing demand or question to sound out their re-actions. "Have you ever thought of selling the business?" "Supposing you made it yourself instead of buying it?" "But you probably could not find $200,000 in ready cash, anyway, could you?" "Have you ever thought about retirement?" These are designed to de-rail the other party from his existing tracks. If you worry him at first with your fishing demand, then leave him alone to get used to the idea, you can then come back to present your plan which appears to him to be very much easier for him than he supposed.

Hint for bargainers:

> Plant the idea, then leave them
> alone with their thoughts.

It is worthwhile being persistent with high demands—but avoid forcing the other party to make a decision if that decision is going to go against you. Once their minds start to move your way, then keep them moving—try to avoid deadlock at this stage. It helps if you have a very sound personal relationship with them.

One of the most unpleasant tasks for a personnel manager is to tell executives that they must take an early retirement. In a food group company, this task was given originally to the financial director. He had a tendency to see the issue in terms of money, pension rights and so on. So he called in the executives, told them about the decision and gave them an analysis of their financial situation showing how the company could arrange things in their favor.

He was one of the most detested men in the business. The long-standing employees were furious, hurt and indignant at the way they were treated. Many of them had been with the company for forty years.

The company hired a personnel manager who changed the system. He would meet the executives casually, in a corridor perhaps, and suggest a meeting later. The meeting was nearly always at the end of the day when both parties could relax. He would ask the executive to consider the company's problems. He would say that things were in a state of flux and that he wanted to get a reaction from the executive before any decisions were made. He told the executive to mull things over and they would have another chat.

In this way, the executives gradually became used to the idea. Many of them actually volunteered themselves for early retirement without realizing that it was to happen to them anyway.

The process took time, but it was entirely effective. The personnel man asked the executives to calculate how the company could best arrange their tax and pension affairs. He offered the help of the financial director in working out the best retirement package for the executive. The executives nearly always accepted this idea, and some were grateful for the company service in this respect.

So when presenting radical ideas the rule is to get the other party used to them first. Try and get him involved in formulating the proposal. Don't be hasty, and make full use of time. If it is going to be difficult for the other party, then let him imagine it to be worse than it turns out to be in the end.

EXPLORATION: PROBING AND PRESENTING

Lighten up your defense
If you want something badly that is your weakness. They might play on it, if you let them discover it. They will probe your defenses and once they find how to get through to you, then they will work on those defenses.

Mr. Agent has judged Mr. Purchase to be a careful man with his money. He is a saver. So he works hard on this motivation.

"As a capital investment, this property will undoubtedly be the most significant deal you have ever made. In monetary terms alone, never mind it being a beautiful house to live in, I will show you how much better off you would be with this rather than with a savings account, life insurance, or a mutual fund. If property values continue to rise, and with the tax situation as it is, I will show you evidence which will prove that this kind of property represents the single best investment decision a man can make today. Look, here are the figures."

The counter to this is to ask him to show you the operating costs. Or if he is showing you the operating costs, ask him how the capital will appreciate. There is always another argument. Find it.

Let's fix the game on the side
This is a tricky technique. The other party takes you confidentially to one side and tries to get you to open up honestly. He suggests that he will tell you what

he wants from the deal, off the record, and you can tell him what you want from the deal, likewise. He says you can both fix it up between you without all these meetings, agents, solicitors, etc. Watch out! As usual he will reveal only what he wants to reveal and he will do so in an apparently candid manner. Don't be fooled.

"I know you are selling the house through an agent," says Mr. Purchase, "but I thought we could save ourselves an awful lot of fuss. I want a house like yours and I've got to do a deal quickly. If we do a deal privately, I can pay you cash, or you tell me whatever it is you want, but I must tell you that the price is too much for me. Think about it, don't forget we could save the agent's fee if we did it just between us. Let me know what you think."

By itself this is not particularly dangerous, although the ethics of cutting out the agent are dubious. But it is dangerous to enter into secret conspiracies with the other party, at their instigation. Listen by all means, but don't reveal yourself.

We've lost the score

This one can catch you unawares at any time. After a particularly long and complex session, they may suddenly tell you they have forgotten what has been agreed earlier. Could you just review it for them? Their object is to make you forget one or more concessions they have made to you, or to make you forget one or other of your demands.

"Oh blast," you'll say later. "We can't go back and ask them for that now." So you will have lost. It is also a technique used for avoiding pressure tactics. When you have them on the run, they can reverse the situation by asking you to summarize the score for them. They are thereby off the hook. And you are on.

"Well, that's about everything so far as the list of fixtures and fittings is concerned. Was there anything else from this morning that we missed, can you remember? Oh well, this is all, then."

SUMMARY

In order to make the other party accept our proposition we must couch it in terms that suit them. The more we know about them and the pressures acting upon them, the better. So it pays the bargainer to be a good listener.

When we shape our case towards the situation of the other party we need to bring him with us, step by step. Having determined his needs and wants, we should then select from our proposition the benefits that will suit the other party best.

It is more effective to ensure that the other party's interest is maintained, by securing his agreement to each point in turn.

Presenting our case through asking questions is a very powerful way of ensuring that it is completely understood. This way the other party convinces himself of our arguments by making connections for himself.

Resistance and Pressure | 8

Complete the following learning module before reading the chapter.

Q.1   *The other party will always test us and our case. He will do this while trying to clarify his thoughts, by showing resistance to what we say, and by putting pressure upon us. The important thing for the bargainer is to determine the intention of the other party. He does this initially by examining the resistance with a RE-DIRECTED question, such as "Why do you say that?" or "What is on your mind?"*

Q.2   *The purpose of asking this .... is to examine the motive behind the resistance. There may be some misunderstanding, for example, which can be quickly cleared up once the other party has been asked to re-state his position.*

Q.3   *Or the other party may be offering an excuse rather than a genuine objection. This may be because he does not want to reveal his true objection, so he must proffer something else instead. The bargainer must always deal with the true objection which may be revealed by his .... He should never answer the excuse. One excuse will simply turn into another one.*

Q.4   *The true objection may not be revealed explicitly by the other party; he may feel that it could expose his hand. (He could have decided to do a deal with someone else, perhaps.) He may be pressing the bargainer to improve his terms. His status may be low (perhaps he himself cannot take the decision). These situations require the bargainer to explore the true objection by means of asking several ...., and to shape his presentation accordingly.*

Q.5   *The asking of a .... also gives the bargainer time to think, and it puts the pressure back on the other party. The bargainer's next objective must be to avoid conflict. There is a simple way of doing this, which is SHOWING AGREEMENT with the other party's right to raise his resistance.*

Q.6   *Human beings are good at counter punching. If A attacks B, then B will attack back. A's renewal attack will be stronger and fiercer. So when B is* *the bargainer, he should deflect the initial attack by .... with the right of the other to raise his question.*

Q.7 *He is not actually agreeing with the resistance itself. What he is doing is to offer sympathy for the other party's point of view even though it may be wrong. By .... through an understanding of their line of thought he can avoid most conflicts while still leaving himself free to adopt whatever position he wants.*

Q.8 *The most familiar technique is for the bargainer first to ask the other party a ...., and then go on to say something like, "Yes, I can see how this might concern you, but don't you think...?" The simple act of .... with the man's point of view will avoid most fights.*

Q.9 *After he has shown himself to be sympathetic to the buyer by .... he then has a variety of techniques available to him. The most effective of these is to turn the resistance into a REASON TO AGREE. This causes the other party's objection to be seen as the very reason why the bargainer's case should be accepted.*

Q.10 *In a way, this means that the bargainer does not see the objection as being an objection at all—instead, by seeing it as a ...., he is using it to support his own case.*

Q.11 *"But that car you are selling me is very costly!" "Yes, of course, and that shows how well-made it is. Reliability is one of the things you want, isn't it?" Or, "I think you are a bit old for this job." "I can see you are probably thinking of all the experience I have had over the years and how useful it will be to have someone who knows what they are doing." This is the way to turn an objection into a ....*

Q.12 *As well as showing them that their resistance is really a good ...., the bargainer could also use a COMPARISON with rival offers, or he could use a THIRD PARTY REFERENCE. Another weak way is to OFFER A TRIAL.*

Q.13 *It is best if the other party can be persuaded to take himself step by step through a .... with rival offers, because in this way he will convince himself. Or quoting a case history of someone else's experience on the same issue, using them as a ...., is another good way. It is generally regarded as a weak maneuver to .... and this should only be done if there is no other way. It is weak because it reduces the bargainer's expectations to the lowest level. He is often willing to accept a small deal as a "successful" result.*

Q.14 *Deal only with that part of their resistance which it is necessary to deal with. Encourage them to make a .... of your offers with others where your case is better or to resolve their particular problem. Quoting from someone else's experience, using this as a ...., means selecting an example of someone who will build up the bargainer's own prestige. The bargainer should only .... if he has secured the other party's commitment to the full deal and all that this means, provided that the trial is a success. And the criterion for success needs to be established from the outset. If the bargainer knows the other party well, and if he is sure of his ground, then he can often REBUT what the other party is saying.*

He should not use this technique relentlessly to answer all their points or resistance. He will annoy them if he does.

Q.15 *If he does .... the case of the other party he should be clear about their objection, otherwise a fight will develop.*

Q.16 *He should also be certain of his ground and be prepared to prove his case if he is to .... their case.*

Q.17 *He should also have built a strong personal relationship with them. If they trust the bargainer, then they will accept it when he does .... their argument.*

Q.18 *A bargainer's case will never be totally superior to a competitor's case on every point. Where there are very many resistances which he can turn to advantage, or objections which he can .... outright, then there will be some parts of his case which do not quite suit the other party or which are weaker than competitor's offerings. Where this happens, he can end by saying IT IS UP TO YOU.*

Q.19 *At the end of a heavy session, he can summarize all the benefits of his case, admit where the weaknesses exist and bring the issue to a close with the statement .... It helps to add one additional benefit after making the statement.*

Q.20 *The point is that the cumulative sum of all his offerings is greater than the occasional weakness and should overwhelm the competitor's case. If the bargainer gets the timing right and says ...., he is recognizing after all what is a fact, and will close many successful deals through doing so.*

Resistance and Pressure | 8

The last thing she expected to receive in the mail was an envelope with 10 twenty-dollar bills in it. And from her husband's manager, too! She hardly anticipated, either, that the end result would be that her husband would leave his job.

The accompanying letter explained that her husband's company was just starting a new sales campaign with an incentive scheme for the wives of the sales agents. The letter explained that management believed that spouses played a great part in their agent's success, and the company had developed this scheme to involve them further. The spouse of the winning agent overall could earn a lot of money—enough for a holiday for the family, or perhaps something towards a small car.

All she had to do was to encourage her husband to achieve high results. The manager's letter said that often a salesman's performance fell off, half-way through a competition when they found they were not winning. With this particular competition, however, each week was a new week, each week she could earn a bonus for herself, and all she had to do was to see that her husband was kept hard at it.

This clearly was pressure. Management was enrolling the spouse as a motivating spur. Pressure is used in all human relationships, from the teasing relationships of children to the power plays of unions and business, to the wars between nations.

In bargaining, each party will always test the other, albeit perhaps gently. They will test each other's integrity: does he deliver what he promises? They will test each other's honesty: can we trust his word? They will test each other's skill: what style does he use in his bargaining? They will test each other's power: does he really need our business badly?

Testing may be done with great subtlety. Take care with the man who is disarmingly honest about himself; he may be pressuring you to reveal confidences about yourself. Take care with the man whose mind wanders everywhere apparently. He may be unsettling you, and checking the consistencies of your answers. Take care with the man who invites you to his home to share his hospitality. He may be increasing his bargaining power and securing your commitment to him. Watch out for the man who shows you his instructions, or tells you something "off the record," or explains the rules to you.

All of these are gentle techniques, so soft that many people would hardly notice them. Each of them may be designed to obtain information about you, or to influence your expectations about the deal, or to exert social control over you. They are designed to increase the other party's power. At the expense of your power.

Tip for bargainers:

The relationship between a man's charm and his wickedness may be direct.

In one way, pressure and resistance are to be welcomed. At least the other party is giving you a feedback. The worst pressure to experience at the start of the bargaining process is complete indifference. Bargainers will always tell you that the man they find most difficult to deal with is the man who does not want to know. He is completely inert to anything they say. He is happy with what he has got and nothing will change his mind. You must make him see a problem before he will move.

Here is the salesman's wife, wondering why she has been sent the money. She reads her instructions.

"Each week your husband has been given a target to achieve. Each is based upon his own performance in a similar period last year, so the targets are quite fair. You can help him by your encouragement. If you can get him off to his first call early, that would be a help. (One more call each day, early in the morning, could add an immediate 15% or more to his results.) And don't be too hard on him if he is home late. After all, if you want that Omni you can buy with the winnings, then you will have to make some sacrifices, too."

The letter is clearly patronizing and quite sexist. Many will be annoyed by it; some husbands and wives could be quite angry. But, despite the aggravation, for most people it will work. It *will* get them going in the morning. The man either gets a new job because he does not like the pressure, or he responds to it.

But why the $20 bills? Here comes the catch. Here is where the screw is turned. This, incidentally, is a case taken from real life.

The letter explained that each wife was given $200 to start with. The scheme would last for ten weeks. At the end of each week, the wives would be told who had scored the highest percentage increase on his sales out of the entire sales team of thirty salesmen. They were given the names and home addresses of all the other wives.

Each wife, each week, had to send one of her $20 bills to the wife of the winning salesman. If the same salesman won the competition every week, then his wife would receive $6000, and the other wives would end up with nothing.

The result of this high pressure tactic? Eight resignations from the sales force; the collapse of the scheme half-way through; the firing of the company sales promotion manager. Two divorces later occurred, in marriages which were a little unsettled before. There was also a rumor that the winning salesman ended up with three wives, but it could not be verified.

Such is the penalty if you put on too much pressure. Catastrophe will result.

There will be a slow build-up of resistance to your pressure. A sticking point will be reached—beyond this point logic and reason will not apply, emotional reactions will take over. And any small trigger can cause catastrophe at this stage. So be warned about using too much pressure.

Tip for bargainers:

> *Press lightly upon emotion,*
> *for you are pressing catastrophe.*

There are three principal means of applying pressure. The first to maintain obvious competition for the deal. The more alternatives you can make available the better—up to a point. Many excellent suppliers will not tender for government or local authority work because they feel there is little chance of getting it.

The second principle is to raise resistance and objections continually. If this is done with personal warmth and encouragement so that hostility does not result, the chances are that the other party will gradually be worn down to their lowest expectations. Always keep the reward in sight for them, and do not allow them to make trade-off concessions to you. They will say, if they are clever, something like: "If I handle that question for you satisfactorily, then do we have a deal?" If you nod at this stage, you lose. It is a closing technique they are using on you. If they try and summarize, making a list of all your objections and asking you if there are any more, then run for the door. Again they are using a closing technique on you. This is to lock you off from thinking up new objections. What should you do about it? Tell them there is another man in your company they'll have to talk to first. Then they will go back to square one.

Thirdly, try to weaken the other party first. It requires careful handling, but if you have an edge on them, it helps. George Harris had to tell the Tesco buying director that they would be losing part of their annual sales discount in the forthcoming year. Harris is the key account negotiator for one of Britain's leading food brands, and Tesco is the company's biggest single account.

What he did first was to complain rather bitterly that during the previous month, December, the Tesco store managers had refused to take deliveries of several thousand cases which had been previously agreed with head office. The buying director was very apologetic and promised to look into it.

Two weeks later, Harris went to see him to tell him about the new discount terms. As he said subsequently, "It was a very rough meeting. They gave me a really hard time. But we got most of what we wanted in the end." He went on to point out that the going would have been much, much worse if they had not felt guilty about the refusals.

Helpful hint for bargainers:

> *Watch out when they do you a favor.*
> *There may be a sucker blow coming.*

COUNTERING PRESSURE

If you know that the other party is going to raise a serious objection to your proposition, then there is one basic rule to follow. Raise the problem yourself in your case to them.

In this way you meet the problem head on, but you can deal with it in your own way, in your own time and under your terms. It shows that you are confident of your case.

Suppose you are selling turkeys to a restaurant. You allow them to say, "But these broiler turkeys have no flavor to them. We don't like them. Freezing damages them." Now you are in some difficulty. It may end up as your view versus their view, with a fight resulting.

Better for you to point out that your broiler turkeys are young, and partly as a result are blander in flavor, just as veal is blander than beef. Also, turkeys in the old days used to be hung for some time to increase their "visceral taint." In other words, when they were sold their insides were slightly rotten, to get that very rich flavor which people don't like so much these days—and neither do health inspectors.

It will not stop their objection, but it will draw the teeth of it.

When they put on the high pressure, then take time to think. Go quiet, and resort to asking questions. Clarify their motives. Ask for further information, ask them to explain themselves. Ask them to tell you what they want. Ask them to tell you what they expect from you. All of this information will help your position and will limit theirs.

You could try avoiding most of the pressure points altogether and just deal with one. By shifting the argument on to your territory slightly, you can explore this at some length and often they will not press you on the rest.

One useful technique during a heated debate is to summarize the situation but to do so incorrectly. This will immediately bring in the other party to correct you and once again the pressure is on them to explain themselves.

A large Danish engineering and construction company was bidding for part of a major Middle East contract held by a German group. Initially they thought they would not land the deal, but gradually they were encouraged by their technical discussions to believe they were ahead of the opposition.

They pressed the issue to a close, but the other party explained that there would be one further meeting. At this last meeting, a senior executive for the Germans led the discussion. He said, "When we ourselves bid for a contract we always leave a little room, just in case. You must do the same thing, we are certain. What I am about to say will hurt, but not a lot. We want the total cost reduced by 12½%. We have put the same proposition to your competitor and we are waiting for his answer. So far as we are concerned there is little to choose between you, but to be honest, we would prefer to deal with you. What do you say?" "We need to talk this over," said the Danes.

The Danish company returned in an hour. They pretended to have misunderstood the Germans. They told them that the specifications could be reduced by the amount wanted and started to list the items which would have to be cut. "No, no," said the Germans. "We want the specifications you have proposed." And the argument then was turned on to the specifications. Never at any time did the Danes respond to the talk of cutting their own price. After an hour of deliberate misunderstandings, the Danes tried to close.

"How much do you want to save?" asked the Danes. The Germans told them. "If we can find these savings for you and maintain the specifications, do we have a deal?" The Germans agreed.

The Danes then showed the Germans how they could alter some of the ways that they, the Germans, were planning to handle the work in order to do it more profitably. The Germans became quite interested. The Danes volunteered to take on some of the German inspection responsibilities as part of their own task. In the end the Germans made the extra profit they wanted, but the Danes conceded hardly anything. They did not panic when the pressure went on. They resisted it. And then they exerted their own control.

The Germans win this end play on four occasions out of five. "It will only hurt a bit" is the nickname of the executive who leads their team.

REDUCING HIGH TENSION

Delay will reduce tension and will calm the atmosphere. You should make use of an adjournment or any other delaying tactic which comes to mind. Refer the matter to someone else, go for a walk, leave it for discussion later—all such delaying techniques can be useful, particularly in conflict bargaining situations.

But other defensive plays are possible. You should always limit the amount of information you reveal under pressure, and rely heavily on your logic. In the face of attack, you must turn the other cheek.

You can fall back on your company policy, you can make a particular issue "non-negotiable," you can claim you lack the authority for the decision, you can make use of an established precedent.

Bargainers should note:

> *In the long run, even non-negotiable*
> *issues can be negotiated.*

Sometimes a third party can be called in. Bring in your boss; or your own expert; ask for an arbitrator. Use the other party's logic against him. Wave a red flag at him so that he can see that you will walk out, withdraw, or do something equally unpleasant unless he modifies his pressure.

If the atmosphere is charged with emotion and tension, then unless you are causing it yourself for a particular reason, you will need time to de-fuse it. Arguments, counterattacks, anger will not help.

PRESSURE TACTICS AND PLAYS

Get their team to play on your side

One individual is often the stumbling block. If you work on the rest of his team, they will bring him along.

Mr. Sells knows that you personally are resisting buying his house, because you really want something smaller and cheaper. Watch out when his wife telephones your wife to ask her around for coffee. The children can play together in the garden, she says—tell them to bring their swimsuits. Mr. Sells is playing the game of getting your team on his side; your family will return to put pressure on you.

Bringing their own referee

Watch out when they bring their own expert with them. He will sit quietly, apparently distance himself from them, and then gradually act as a referee. His position is apparently independent of both parties. But he isn't. He is on their side—he just lets you think he isn't.

Mr. Purchase comes to have another look at your house and tells you that someone else is due to arrive shortly, do you mind?

"He has come to have a look at the woodrot position," he says. "There isn't any woodrot," you say. "But there might be in the future," he says. Watch out.

When the expert turns up, he will hum and hah, telling you both that the damage has not gone so far as to be noticeable to the untrained eye, and luckily it will only cost $1,000 to take preventive action now. Then he leaves. Mr. Purchase turns to you and suggests you both split the difference. The cost to you? $500.

The counter play to this is to refuse to let their expert take the chair. Leave them alone together; don't talk with their man at all; don't be around when he gives them advice. Don't bargain with their expert. Bargain only with the amateur on woodrot—Mr. Purchase. Or bring your own expert.

Let's both play against him

Take care when the other party starts talking about your deadly enemy. He may be roping you in to a game where you both play against the bogey man.

"I'll be quite honest with you," says Mr. Purchase. "I really would prefer your neighbor's house. It's much better for us in a number of ways. I know this sounds silly, but I don't really like the man, do you? He seems a rather obnoxious type. I'd rather do a deal with you than with him, if you can just match his terms. It would be one in the eye for him, if you could sell your house first, wouldn't it?"

The counter to this is for you, apparently, to like everyone in the world equally as well as everyone else. Your only bogey man is your bank manager, who does not like it if you give money away....

You can't have the last goal

Be careful of getting too excited. The other party can bounce you at the end, if you do. During the session they will agree to some concession which pleases you. But right at the end, when you are ready to sign, they will find some reason to withdraw it. This is a high pressure tactic, one which can cause serious rows and charges of unfair play, but if they get their timing right, then you will concede.

Mr. Sells has agreed to include the dining-room suite as part of the deal. You wanted this badly because your wife liked it, your own suite is not suitable for the room and Mr. Sells is getting a new one anyway. Right at the end, he says, "Oh, I'm so sorry, but my wife won't let the dining-room suite go because she had already promised it to our daughter. I did not know this." (It is always someone else's fault; there is always a communications problem; and there is always an apparently good reason.)

The counter to this is to cost out the value of the original concession, price it high, and knock it off the total price you pay, with a "take it or leave it" closure. They'll deal.

Don't let them direct your game

Watch out when they summarize the situation. They may include items which you have not conceded or upon which argument has not concluded. If they get away with this at the review stage, then if you try and pick it up later, they will cry "Foul!"

"Let's see where we have got to," said Mr. Purchase. "You want $300,000, which will include the house and the fixtures, the grounds, the swimming pool, I take it that the garden shed is included, and the greenhouse, the garden furniture, but look—what are you going to do about the fittings, such as the lights and shades and things like that? Are they included?"

Watch out, you have just conceded the garden furniture, including the bar-becue, the chairs and outdoor table, sunbeds, and half a dozen items of sundry equipment you were planning to take with you.

The counter to this is for you to do the summary yourself.

We are not going to play with you any more

Probably the strongest pressure technique is the walk-out. They may be bluffing, but they may not. If they are bluffing then they may have to find a way to come back but without losing face. They may mean it at the time, but they can also regret it later. So if withdrawal occurs, with no agreement to meet again, you may have to let them go, but try and keep a door open. You may have to make a face-saving concession to get them back; it could be their embarrassment which holds them away from you later.

"I'm sorry," says Mr. Sells. "But we are not getting anywhere like this. You are pushing me too hard. I'll find another buyer. Good-bye." And he goes.

Let him go, but make sure that you repair as much as you can of the personal relationship between you. This has probably been damaged. Admit you have been too hard. Appreciate his position. Congratulate him on standing up to you. Tell him that while he is sleeping on it, you will do the same. Perhaps something can be worked out, who knows?

Time will begin to work on your side now. Ask him later to meet you socially, but do not discuss business at all. Say that you think it is better to keep off the subject. Whatever you do, don't play the hard man again. He will finish with you for ever, if you do. Just let him come along by himself. It may take several social meetings. In the end he will come down to what you want, unless he develops a better alternative. In this case your position becomes suddenly very weak indeed. He and his new-found customer may now combine to play "Let's both play against him"—but against you.

Bringing in their reserves when you are exhausted

In the Middle East, the favorite trick is to invite the European supplier around to see the sights during the heat of the day, and to take him to a night club and floor show. Around midnight the group is joined by the other party's team leader. He is fresh and his mind is alert. He won't admit it, but he has been asleep most of the evening. He catches the European suppliers around 3 a.m. That's when the big concessions are made. Only one party is exhausted. The loser.

You have nearly tied up the deal with Mr. Purchase. He invites you and your wife to a show and to supper afterwards, but initially only his wife turns up, and explains that there is a crisis, but her husband will show up later—which he does. But he will not discuss business; he seems rather withdrawn about it, you begin to be afraid that he will not do the deal after all. Around 11 p.m. he begins to reveal his serious problem. He does not know how to say this. He says you cannot help, but it is his problem.

"You must tell us," you say. "I cannot raise the full mortgage," he says. Then he goes quiet, says nothing. You offer to help in any way you can. He cannot see how. You ask him to be precise. He tells you that when he has put everything together, all that he can scrape up, he is still $1,000 short. In the end, you will fall for the game. You will end up paying for the evening out—about $500 is the usual price.

The counter? Socialize with them after the deal is concluded, and not before. Explain that for medical reasons your doctor insists you are in bed by midnight/ not allowed to drink/forbidden to look at beautiful women/devoted to marital fidelity.

Let the managers play together

Sometimes they will press you by saying that their boss is threatening to call your boss.

"Look," says Mr. Sells, "We are not getting anywhere with this. My wife gets on with your wife, why don't we let them sort it out?"

Just make sure you call your boss first and tell him/her what is going on. Tell him/her to make much tougher demands than you have been making. That will frighten off their boss, and they'll be pleased to deal with you, because you seem more reasonable.

SUMMARY

When bargainers meet they will test out each other. They will test each other's honesty and they will search for the weaknesses in each other. Sometimes the pressure may be quite severe, in order to force out the issues or press the bargainer down.

The first step in handling such pressure is to avoid argument and to seek to clarify the issue. Asking the other party to explain their points more fully is one way of reducing the tension, clarifying the issue, and also buying time to think.

Argument should be avoided. Sometimes a third party story can be used to indicate how someone has overcome the problem; on other occasions the objection raised can itself be turned into a reason for doing the deal.

No case ever offers 100% perfection to the other party. Admitting some weaknesses in one's own case may be a sensible maneuver.

In general, resistance may be no bad thing. It can show where the other party has misunderstood us, or it can reveal his needs and the direction of his thinking.

Handling Price | 9

Complete this questionnaire before reading the chapter. Complete it again after reading the chapter. Then turn to the answers at the end of the book to find out your score.

Q.1   *You are a trade union negotiator at the first round of the annual wage bargaining. Inflation is running at 5%, and the other unions are getting about 7% on average, with the top awards around 10%. At the first meeting do you:*
(a) *submit a demand for 12%;* (b) *ask them for their offer;* (c) *suggest you can work out ways of improving productivity so as to get 15%;* (d) *say you will accept 7% but they must guarantee no lay-offs?*

Q.2   *They say they are not prepared to formulate any offer yet because the company is doing badly, and they must get the productivity increased. They show you the evidence for this and it is apparently true. You know there are many areas where you can help to increase efficiency and save costs. Do you:*
(a) *say you will discuss productivity only if they agree to a satisfactory wage settlement beforehand;* (b) *submit your demand for 12% with any productivity deal extra on top;* (c) *say you will not bargain without an offer of theirs being on the table first;* (d) *submit ideas for improving productivity one by one, with your members sharing the benefits each time?*

Q.3   *You are the lawyer for a company defending an action brought by a supplier who is suing for non-payment of a disputed account. When you know there is to a court hearing, do you:*
(a) *suggest you meet the other party's lawyer privately to discuss how the matter might be settled out of court;* (b) *ask for a breakdown of the other party's costs;* (c) *tell them you will defend the action all the way through appeals, because your client is incensed at their behavior (although you plan to see if a deal is possible outside the courtroom door);* (d) *suggest to your client that he make them a good offer now to save all the legal costs involved in the dispute?*

Q.4 *You are the agent for an international golf star whose reputation is on the wane. He hit the jackpot once but became involved in too many promotions, played too much exhibition golf, and charged about the world scooping in the money. His fee now is only half of the fee charged by top pros today. He has not been invited to compete by the sponsors of the Spanish Open. You call up the company and they ask you what he charges. Do you:*
(a) tell them that his low fee is because he wants to visit Spain; (b) remind them of his past winnings, and quote them the fee; (c) explain that you realize they have a great many costs to bear and his little fee will not add to them very much; (d) don't tell them his fee, if you can help it; (e) ask them how much they expect his fee would be?

Q.5 *You are the skipper of a tug, operating in a force 10 storm. A Greek freighter is in serious trouble with engine failure and is being pressed on to a rocky lee coast. If you can take him in as salvage, you and your crew can divide up the proceeds, but you have to get the Greek skipper to agree first. He might stay aboard and try to save her himself. You radio him. Do you:*
(a) tell him that with the insurance money he can get a new ship. (He can't. And he is under-insured, probably); (b) tell him that in your personal view his ship is doomed without your help, because you know these shores well; (c) explain that you've just had a message from your owners to tell you to break off to avoid damage to your own ship, and he must come now or never; (d) explain that his ship would be going to the breaker's yard in three years anyway, by salvaging her now it would lose him perhaps $100,000 profit. That is only $50 a day profit after tax. Does he want to risk his life for the sake of his company earning $50 a day profit, compared to picking up the insurance in a lump sum now?

Q.6 *Bribery. What is your general attitude to it?*
(a) Revulsion —would never engage in it under any circumstances; (b) can't be quite as definite as this, but cannot envisage many circumstances where you would condone it; (c) if it's a question of take it or leave it, you'd rather take it; (d) general enthusiasm.

Q.7 *You are in a taxi in Zwala, Burumba. The taxi driver suddenly stops the car and runs away. Two big Burumban policemen get in and sit on either side of you. They begin to talk to each other, not about you, but about their Burumban prisons. They do not answer your questions. You cannot get out of the taxi. Have your views now altered from the previous question?*
(a) Will you never engage in bribery under any circumstances? (b) can you now envisage a circumstance where you could condone it? (c) are you prepared to go along with the policemen's own ideas on the subject? (d) could you be quite enthusiastic now about your participation?

Q.8   *What do you say after naming your price?*
(a) Nothing at all, you keep quiet; (b) add one more little benefit; (c) ask
them for their opinion; (d) ask them for the business; (e) tell them your
terms of business?

Score   **Score**
___   ___

Before reading chapter.   *After reading chapter.*

___   ___

Handling Price | 9

Suppose that next Monday you were to receive a letter with a Hong Kong postmark, inviting you to run a one-day seminar for the Hong Kong Management Association. The letter is signed by their Director General. He is asking you to handle a program for him on a topic which is entirely familiar to you. He will make all the arrangements, do the advertising and get the people there. You would like to do it.

He has offered to pay your traveling expenses both ways, and will pay for your stay at a five-star hotel and any other out-of-pocket expenses. He wants to know simply this: how much will you charge him as a fee for handling the day's program?

This question is posed at a management seminar on the topic of pricing strategy. The audience is asked to write down the answers, which usually vary from about $500 for the day up to $5,000 or more. Some managers are willing to do it for nothing just for the experience of going to Hong Kong. Those quoting low figures are those who want to do the work and the fee is not important to them. By pricing it low they imagine they will get the work. They are quite wrong in this belief.

Those at the top end of the scale do not care whether they go or not. They say to themselves: "If this man has gone to the trouble of getting in touch with me, then presumably he will be willing to pay a high price." So two pricing principles are emerging immediately. The first is that if you badly want to do the work, then you will price it down. The second is that if you know the other party badly wants you to do the work, then you can price it up.

The more a bargainer can arouse the interest and the enthusiasm of the other party in his proposition, the less difficulty he will have over his price.

Bargainers should note:

> *There is only one "right" price, and*
> *that is what the customer is willing to pay.*

In the seminar the screw is now turned a little. The audience is told that the Hong Kong Management Association have written to other experts around the world to lead this one-day seminar. The total range of fees they have been quoted stretch from nothing in the case of the man who wants to go to Hong Kong anyway, to $5,000. Now the managers know that the work is competitive, will they change their own quoted price—if so, how?

What happens now is interesting. Remember that their prices are pulled out of the air originally—based upon little else than straw indications of cost and value. Yet most managers will not alter their price, even though they know that this will lose them the work, and they also know their own decisions were arbitrary! So here is another factor about price. People dig in their heels, and hard. They are not flexible enough on the issue.

But some managers in the audience do change their quoted price when they know what the competition is up to. Those at the top end of the scale start to reduce their demands (they feel they are trying to take too much), and those at the bottom end of the scales raise their prices (they feel that their low price is weak). The mean average of all the prices quoted by the audience rises somewhat.

The greatest anxiety is shown by the managers who feel they are pricing themselves too low. They feel themselves to be in a position of weakness—and this reflects the truth. Low price is associated with low quality, in the other party's mind.

Bargainers take heed:

> *The lowest price of all carries the seeds*
> *of its own destruction.*

The tail is now to be twisted a little. The managers are asked to imagine themselves now to be the Director General in Hong Kong. Which quote should they accept? They have the same information available about everyone—the only difference is the price. There is only one constraint, they are not allowed to pick their own quotation; they are forced to go either higher or lower.

When they are acting in the role of the buyer, they can see that profit is not the sole motivation which drives him on. He is interested also in not losing money—a far different matter. He is interested in having a good program run, one which will keep his own members happy. There is a risk for him in hiring someone who is too low in price—perhaps the person is no good. Equally, there is risk in hiring the highest priced person—maybe this is a rip-off. So in general, when they are acting out the role of buyers, the managers plump for the middle range of quotes—but the average fee is again raised slightly. It is a little higher than the median average quoted by the same audience when they were in competition for doing the work.

The buyer is seeking reassurance from having a slightly higher price, but he does not want it to be so high that it loses contact with reality. He might pay the absolute top price for an international "star" speaker with a reputation, but he will not pay this for an unknown.

So we see that the proper approach to price lies often in the area of behavior analysis, rather than in precise forms of cost measurement. In any segment of the market, price is associated with ideas of "value for money," high prices search out and find high value customers who are willing to pay the price in return for quality. Low prices equally search out different customer groupings altogether. These are concentrated more on questions of low cost in return for adequate performance.

Pricing issues are less sensitive when there is a high degree of variation in the products and services being offered. Then a wide choice of prices prevails. Where products and services are narrowly different from each other, where the buyer is experienced and purchases these things many times over, then the difference between competitive prices will be small. So if you want to get a higher price than the competition, then you have got to get more leverage— and you must deal with the right customer. You must sell him on your benefits first, arouse his interest and his enthusiasm, and then give him the price.

But the converse applies if you are a buyer. Stop them from quoting their benefits at you. Just get them to give you the price, first of all. Imagine that price is the one and only thing which matters to you. This will force down their expectations and they will give you their best price. But take care that you do not pin them down on some specified part of a contract, leaving yourself open to them loading the bill on services which have not been estimated in advance.

Farmers are usually tough and cunning bargainers. So distributors of agro-chemicals get a hard time. One distributor adds a great deal of technical service and advice for his customers so his prices tend to be higher. He does not want to lose out all the time on the big orders, so he has trained his sales office staff as follows. When the farmer rings up and says: "Give me your best price on cereal weed control products," the telephone salesclerk answers immediately with "Certainly, sir, our very best price is…" and this is generally lower than the competition. The farmer is delighted, but the clerk goes on: "This price, sir, is for 10 ton lots, you collect, and cash in advance." The farmer is taken aback. But generally he remains talking and will provide more information to the telephone clerk if he asks. Initially he was not willing to tell him anything.

No farmer wants to accept these terms, and the distributor does not win on all the cut price deals. But he does manage to turn a few of the bargain hunters into responsible and sensible customers with whom he establishes a relationship. The distributor gets into a negotiating situation this way. When the farmer demurs at the terms, the clerk says, "What price are you looking for? Why don't I send one of our representatives around to see you?" It often does work, and business results from it.

When the representative calls on the farmer he asks him how much he would like to save on his costs. "$2,000? $4,000?" He gets the farmer to agree that if he, the representative, can find ways of the farmer saving even more money than he is thinking of, then the farmer will give him the business. The representative surveys the farm and the methods. He is a technical specialist. He is certain to know of a few wrinkles here and there which can save the farmer money, often quite a lot of money. The farmer is impressed. And the representative has proved what a valuable service the farmer is paying for. Over the years it can be worth far more than a little bargain hunting ever will.

Price cannot be divorced from other factors in the business. Everything a company does has a cost attached to it. By altering the methods, by changing the circumstances, a different deal can be done. And that is the job of the bargainer—to look for alternative means of handling the work together which have cost benefits for both parties.

If price becomes a sticking point as it often does, then there is a simple solution for the bargainer. The deal has to be altered in some way. Most deals can be reconstructed so that the other party gets more of what he wants, and so do we. If what he wants is a low price, then something costly must come out of the specification or he must help our costs in some way. Or perhaps we can change the way the deal is priced. Most people running seminars in Hong Kong will settle for a flat fee per day. But other people do it on a profit-sharing basis, or charge a fee per head, or do other work on the way in places such as Singapore and Manila and share the costs, or they use the occasion to drum up extra business for themselves from other sources in Hong Kong, or they do a reciprocal deal, or they try and get paid in Swiss francs, or cash. There are a thousand ways of getting what we want from any deal. The best ways are always through identifying what the other party wants as well, and then building that into the deal.

Once the mind opens up to new possibilities, the great profit opportunities are revealed. The trouble with price is that it fixes both buyer and seller into a straitjacket from which neither party finds it easy to extricate himself. This is particularly true in very repetitive situations in long-established industries. People are very uncreative in the area of price.

Rely on costs only in so far as they give you the bottom line, the price below which you dare not go, and remember that the "price" can be cut a thousand different ways. The purpose of the price bargainer is to find the complex of ways which will suit the other party.

Circular logic for bargainers:

> *If they press you on price, tell them about the quality.*
> *If they press you on quality, tell them about the service.*
> *If they press you on service, tell them about the terms.*
> *If they press you on terms, tell them about the price.*

Presenting price arguments

The first rule of bargaining remains, on price as on all else—if you don't have to bargain, don't bargain. So put the price statement firmly as if there is no moving from it. If you signal with words such as "about" or "hear" or "roughly," they will take this to mean that you can go lower. And follow the other rule of bargaining—ask for more than you expect to get, because you may need the room.

Perhaps you can get the other man to tell you first what he expects. Fred Rogers is a sales manager for a tanning company based in New Jersey. He was seeing a customer about a new product which the company had produced which was to be sold in strips for processing to leather manufacturers. By touching this particular customer's vanity, Fred Rogers made over $5,000 more than he expected.

This customer could be difficult when he wanted, as Fred knew. The customer was a kidder—he joked with Fred about his company, his product, his management. "What do you think of it, then?" said Fred.

"Well, I quite like it, but I expect you are now going to tell me that it is very expensive and that I should pay a ridiculous price for it. I've heard it all before from you people," said the customer.

"You tell me," said Fred. "You are an experienced man in the trade. You know leather and hide as well as anyone. How much would you expect it to cost?"

The man was flattered, and replied that he thought it would cost probably about 45 cents a yard. "You are right on," said Fred Rogers, with an amazed look. "I don't know how you do it. How did you guess?"

The sales manager got his order at the price of 45 cents a yard and repeat business followed. Both parties were pleased at the outcome of events, even the customer. Fred never did tell him that the product was originally priced by his company at 39 cents a yard.

Present the price at the end, after the benefits of the proposition have been explained and the other party is enthusiastic for the deal. Sandwich the price in between two benefits, and don't pause. If you pause, then he will raise a price objection—that's why you must have something to say after naming the price, preferably one last benefit.

Tip for bargainers:

> *If you stop for breath after naming*
> *your price, then you will let him in.*
> *You might not get your breath back.*

When you present him with the price you must make it look small, so break it up into chunks. But when you present him with his profits, you must make them look big, so amalgamate them together.

One pharmaceutical company sells a particularly expensive drug to veterinary surgeons. The price looks terrible when compared to the competition. So the salesmen ask the vets how many doses they can get out of a pack of the product. Then they show them by using their own product they are only spending an extra 3 cents per cow, which is nothing really, is it? But if they were to say it was $30 per pack extra, then that sounds like a lot.

You can also spread the price thin, extending over time. The seller of bridles and harnesses for horses explains that his products will last for five years at least, of very hard wear. "That's less than $2 a week, and could easily be less than 50 cents if you keep it in good condition, so that it lasts longer." The full price of the equipment is $500.

You must justify the price, because otherwise they may think you are cheating them. Show them the expensive features, the high-priced material. The world's largest makers of filter paper for use in laboratories sell some sheets for certain kinds of tests which cost about 30 cents each. That seems very high for a small piece of paper, so the salesman asks the prospect how much he thinks prime beef steak costs. Between them they work it out at $20,000 a ton or more. "Do you know that we have to pay $22,000 a ton for the glass fibre materials which are used in this product?" he asks. "That is more than the cost of steak, even before we start making the product."

When presenting, always have in mind a competitor who is priced above you, and quote him relentlessly. Because he is high priced, then he will be associated with high quality in the buyer's eyes. It must be good for you to be compared to a Rolls-Royce. At the same time you can show the prospect that you are cheaper than the competitor.

That will help to counter his arguments which are being used against you. He will always tell you of competitors who are lower than you in price. That is the way he thinks, that is his job, that is what his experience has taught him to do. Don't give in to him. Get him on to your comparison with the higher-priced competitor.

Helpful hint for bargainers:

> *Tell him you never mind low-priced competitors,*
> *because they must know what they are worth.*

Miniaturize the price differences between your proposition and what he is doing at the moment, if you are proposing something more expensive. Ask him how much he is paying now. Establish clearly the actual difference between the competitor and yourself and do not be afraid of it. Then work on the difference, not on the total cost. Ask him how much he uses of the material in each item of product that he makes. (Or how often he uses it. Or how much he uses at a time. Find any way you like to break his usage down into small pieces.) Then show the cost of your proposition by comparison in the same pieces. "For how many hours a day do you use your present fork lift truck? Six and a half? Well if you buy ours, then you get all this extra maneuverability, this greater loading capacity and this safer and more comfortable driving position for only 6 cents per hour over the life of the machine." (Actually your machine costs over $1,000 more than the one they have at present.) "That will cost you only an extra $20 on your monthly budget—you cannot grumble at that, can you?"

There are alternative ways of minimizing cost. You can then go on to show the equivalent spending. "What else can you buy for $20 a month, a meal for two in an ordinary restaurant?" "Even if you took the cash difference of $1,000 what could you do with the money? You could just about buy half a truck tire for that—and it would last you half the time."

You could show them the cost penalties of not buying.

"The trouble is that if you leave it for a year, then the price will have gone up by about $1,200 anyway. Not only that, but you will have to keep the same layout in your warehouse, so you will have to go on using outside storage until you buy our machine which will allow you to use the extra storage capacity. I reckon it must be costing you an unnecessary $2,000 a year. Better for you to deal now."

Making objections about price

The buyer is often faced by salesmen who will give the impression that they have no discretion on price. Our prices and discounts, they say, are non-negotiable. Don't fall for it.

The first rule of buying is to find out if they have any discretion and then get it from them. You should start with price and hold them on it. They will try to keep the price until later. Don't let them, they are only trying to get you excited. Separate the price as a discrete issue by itself. Use check comparisons against other prices. It pays you to be well prepared in this and to have done your homework.

The skillful buyer will distance himself at first from the other party and obtain a range of competitive prices. After that, he will be dealing from strength, checking the competitive specifications face-to-face with the other party. As the other party puts the benefits of his proposition, then he can put the comparative weaknesses. The buyer can show competitive quotations if he likes, but he must be careful of his reputation if he does so. He could be accused of revealing confidential information and it will disturb many suppliers to the point of withdrawing from the discussion.

A private buyer wanted a new small Fiat car for his wife. First he waited until the market was quiet, until late November. Then he searched around the dealers to find out who had extra stocks of the model he wanted. He telephoned three dealers for their best price. Most of them would not commit themselves, quite properly, but he sensed that he could get about $300 off a car retailing at $5,000.

Then he broke the rule which says you should go to the man at the top if you want more. He reckoned that if he dealt with his chosen dealer's manager, he would be dealing with a hard man. So he went in casually to a branch where a sales assistant was in charge. He explained that he was just about to sign up a deal with a competitor who had given him a very special offer. He said this competitor had excess inventory and was a bit anxious to clear them. He also said that with interest charges running above 20% per annum it was costing them about $400 to keep a car in stock for six months. He said he was sure he couldn't get a better deal and he prepared to walk out. He had kept the conversation light. The sales assistant asked him how much he was looking for. He told her $800. She asked him to hold the decision until she had spoken to her manager. The buyer got the car at $700 off the usual price. The assistant had worked on her own manager because she wanted the sale.

Hint for buying bargainers:

> *You must get them excited, too, if they*
> *are to do the best deal for you.*

A really skilled car salesman will always win against the private buyer. He does two car deals every week of his life, and the buyer buys a car every few years. The car salesman must be stronger simply because of his experience.

One of the big problems in selling cars is to handle the window shopper who is just searching around for the best trade-in deal. One salesman, when he realizes that a customer is "just looking for the best price," refuses to give his price. What he does is to take out his business card, write the customer's name on it, together with a figure which he does not disclose to the customer. He pins the card on the wall of his office. He tells the customer that this figure "is the best deal you can possibly get." He advises him then to talk with other dealers and when he has done so to come back and see what price he has written on the card.

Practically everyone comes back because they are intrigued. The figure written down is not the best deal, but the salesman is not taken aback. "What deal have you been offered, sir?" he asks, and nearly always the customer tells him. Then, at that point the salesman knows where he stands. He has a serious prospect, and he is fairly confident of the competitor's price. He can now choose to do a deal or not, as the case may be. He sells many cars every year.

Ask them for cost breakdowns. If they are daft enough to give them to you, then you can play the game of working their arguments against themselves. Somewhere, somehow, their costs will not add up. You have opened up a Pandora's box of options for yourself. You can trap them by asking them for the cost of some particular feature. Wait until they tell you. Then say you don't want it, and can they knock it off the total bill?

While they quote you prices, and give you cost breakdowns, you should refuse any commitment. If you are not careful, they will begin to close you down. They will spot any extra interest of yours, see it as a buying signal, and begin to work on it.

Buy yourself time to think; use delay. But don't irritate them so much that they can see you are going to be a difficult man, because if they lose interest in dealing with you, you will not get the best deal. Use personal warmth and secure a friendly relationship. Don't let a price discussion become heavy. As a buyer, you should not hammer them, otherwise they will dig in.

Keep the conversation loose and open. Take it into other areas, under your control. Break off for lunch, talk to them about their business (not yours).

Note to selling bargainers:

Don't let them take you to lunch
to talk about your business.

Add up the total profit contribution they are likely to earn from the deal, and begin gently to float this into their minds. Just as they are trying to make you see how much profit there is in the deal for you, so you can let them see how much profit there is in the deal for them.

Get the timing right. When you are ready, summarize. Make sure that their interest is high at the time. Then tell them what you want. Give them your big demand just once. Let them go away and become used to the idea. Leave the door open and ensure that you "sell" them on the idea of meeting your demands. Introduce financial arguments into your case to them.

Point out the value to them of clearing their inventory/improving their cash position/ making room for more production/ keeping their labor employed/ improving their prestige/ improving their market position—and so on.

Whatever you do, always ask them what the cost is going to be. Otherwise you will be in for a "buy now—bargain later" game.

Tip for bargainer buyers:

> *If you don't ask them how much they are*
> *going to charge you, then they will charge*
> *you all they possibly can.*

Handling objections about price

If you are making a selling proposition, then try to structure the situation so that you get few objections from the other party about price. Timing is important. If you can press them at the right time, just when they need what you have, then they will give you less trouble on price.

When you next see a report of a fire in a hotel, then you can be assured that groups of business-hungry negotiators will be circulating in the area within twenty-four hours. There will be a group of executives from fire alarm systems companies; another group from security companies; a further group from insurance companies; a group of local builders specializing in fire prevention systems. All they need to get their market going for them is a good fire in the area.

They must land the business quickly, within three weeks, otherwise the memory of it will fade and hotel proprietors will settle down again. But if they catch the moment right, then they will do the business and they will get their asking price.

If the buyer is giving you a difficult time over your price, you should stand firm for a long time before making any significant concession. The harder you fight for what you want at the start, the less you will give away in the long run. But if they get you running early on, they'll keep you running.

They will give you all sorts of excuses which you will find difficult to break. "We are committed to this now, so this is all the money we have got." "We have nothing left in our budget." "We are already overspent." "Where am I going to find that kind of money?"

Probe their cash position. Cash flows into and out of a business in different strengths at different times of the year. If you want to get money from the retail clothing trade then don't try it in December. They are stocked up with Christmas and winter sale lines. Try it in late January, after the sale. That's when the money pours in. But March is no good, because they have taken in their spring stocks and cash is short again.

Often you can overcome a price objection by making it seem very easy for them to pay. For most men, paying out $300 more for a suit is rather nasty. But for a man to pay a sum of money into an account each month is easier, because then he can simply dip into his account, draw on a little credit, and it does not seem to matter to him when he buys his suit.

Many a deal has been closed on the terms of the payments period rather than the total sum itself.

Sometimes the buyer's need for the business will be very strong. The seller can spot the opportunity to raise his price to the highest level. Be careful when using this sort of leverage. If it is a one-shot deal, and the two parties will never see each other again, then use this lever to get a high price. Be prepared for considerable resentment and possible welshing on the deal, particularly if the man thinks afterwards he has been cheated.

With a collaborative bargaining possibility, however, play it long. Do not agree immediately to the business. Tell them that if you do it, then the normal rates will apply but that you are interested only in longer-term business. Ask them what they can do for you in this respect. And then tie them down to an agreement on this issue before agreeing to supply the emergency need. Do not do big favors for people without getting a corresponding favor in return. And do not go for the immediate short-term profit opportunity when you could develop a much bigger one in the long run.

Bribes

It is easy to say "do not take them and do not give them." Unfortunately business would not be able to operate at all on a multinational basis in some countries of the world if negotiators did not conform to local cultural conditions.

It is obnoxious to our Western culture; it offends us. We often have an emotional reaction against any kind of corruption. Bribing is not to be condoned in any way because it ruins the fabric of ordered economic society.

Advice for bargainers:

> *Don't get into a position where you may have to
> bribe your way out of corruption charges.*

There seems to be a scale of acceptable morality. Few people object to a salesman's commission or an incentive scheme. But what happens when customers are roped into the incentive scheme also? If they help the salesman with leads to new business they might be rewarded. Is this morally acceptable?

How about rewards to customer's staff; competitions and such like? Or how about the practice of giving prizes to customers, or a bottle of Scotch at Christmas? So far, few people would complain about the ethics involved.

How about the conventions held in Monte Carlo, with the customer given $1,000 in chips to play the tables? Ah, most people would say that this is close to the bone.

How about working in some countries of South America where you have to bribe practically everyone to get any personal service at all? If you don't do it, you won't get anywhere. On some airlines it makes no difference whether you have confirmed your ticket or not. Those who have tipped the right person get on the plane. All others go on the waiting list. What is your view of bribery now while it is 100°F in the shade and the next plane is two days away?

Bribery is built into the structure of some economic systems. The common device is to disguise it in some form such as "agents commission" and to be rather less than rigorous in tracing where and how such commission is paid.

Corruption is signalled to the bargainer in some way. The usual way is by simple delay. Nothing happens. The bargainer is waiting day after day in his Jakarta hotel room for a meeting with a high official and nothing happens. "Ah," says someone in "the know." "You should see his friend first, perhaps." You meet his opaque friend and find yourself having an abstruse conversation. He will not allow you to link the issue of paying money directly to a meeting with the official. If you try to do this, he will withdraw. But you will be left with an understanding, as to how it should be paid, how much, where and when.

The trouble with bribery is that it seeps into the fabric of the relationship like acid. It distorts values, it makes people buy things for reasons other than need or sense; it also breeds cynical bargainers who believe that everyone is on the make. Actually, in the Western world, very few people are. Most people in advanced economies will be horrified at being presented with an open bribe— it is so alien to their experience.

The best advice for the bargainer is the same as for making any concession. If you don't have to, then don't. Wait until they make their move, then respond slowly, if at all. Make sure you have the right signals from the right man. Do your homework; check up with other suppliers and people working in the market. The process will sort itself out. Have patience.

BARGAINING ON PRICE: TACTICS AND PLAYS

The offside trap
This is a sweet play. Here they focus on just one feature of your proposition. They ask how much it costs and then tell you they do not want it, so you have to drop the price.

"Does your price include all those cans of paint and garden equipment in the garage?" asks Mr. Purchase. "Oh yes," you reply, "that's all included."

"How much is all that worth then, do you think?"

"About $500 probably."

"Well we don't want it, we've got our own paint and garden equipment. You can sell it, and I take it you'll knock off $500 from the price." You've been caught in an offside trap.

The counter to this is to refuse to give him a cost breakdown. Or if you do, then you must ask him first if he is interested in buying the paint and equipment in the garage, because you can then give him a favorable price for it. That will stop his play.

We'll hold the kitty
Watch out for cash-up-front demands. And never offer it to them voluntarily

in order to finance their costs. Who do you think you are—a banker? If they need money, let the banks give it to them. The banks know how to screw them down tight so that they do not run away with it. But you don't.

THE KAMIKAZE HOUSE SELLER

You want $100,000 for your house? We've just seen one for $90,000. What do you say to that?

We must sell it quickly because we are desperate to move.

Oh, we cannot get a loan for more than about $80,000. How does that affect you?

That's terrible news, because you are the only buyer we have seen.

Of course, the loan would have to include the carpets, and curtains, ...

No one seems interested in this kind of property.

... garden furniture, all the tools in your garage, the lawnmower, ... are you going to take the rabbit with you?

It's been on the market for years.

That leaves about $40,000 for the house itself. I take it that will be acceptable to you?

Yes, please.

You are a hard man to do business with.

"Here are our terms for handling your house sale," says Mr. Agent. "We take the normal 5% commission, which is payable half on exchange of contract and half on completion (which *isn't* normal), and we will look after the entire responsibility for advertising your house, looking after sales prospects, getting you the best price, all included in the commission, apart from you paying us in advance for the advertising costs. Incidentally, our service to you includes all the telephone calls at our own cost, and you won't find hidden extras."

What you will find is that you have paid him for the advertising up front.

Of course if you are selling, then it is perfectly in order to try and hold the kitty if you can. But don't call it cash up front. It does not sound nice. Call it "financing your front end costs." That sounds a lot better.

Buy now—bargain later
This tactic can be used by both buyers and sellers. The buyer will often offer future business promises if only the seller will do him a favor now. After the

favor has been done, the talks on future business become stalled. That's one ploy.

Sellers use it on buyers with a strong need. They get the buyer's initial authorization on the job, then the buyer finds that he cannot escape, or that he is committed to a service or maintenance contract, or to an open-ended price.

"How much will your services cost?" Mr. Sells asks his lawyer. "My usual conveyancing charge," is the reply, "plus out-of-pocket expenses."

"How much will these be?"

"How can we tell that until we have completed the deal?"

Or, here is another example. "How much do you charge for doing a complete house survey?"

"$15 an hour."

"How long will you spend on doing the survey, then?"

"How can we tell that until we have done the survey? It depends on what we find. Just sign here."

Consultants who charge out on a rate per day basis have been known to charge out ten-day weeks. There are a million little ways in which "Buy now—Bargain later" works. Every contract has some open-check element about it. Just take care, and read the small print.

Let's both play to these rules

Never sign their forms. If you do, you are playing to their rules. And when their rules were drawn up, the Marquess of Queensberry was on their payroll.

"I am not allowed by law to act on your behalf until I have a formal authorization from you," says Mr. Agent. "It does not involve you in anything except signing on this line. It's a standard document. Everyone we deal with signs it. We can start as soon as the ink is dry. You'd like us to get going on your behalf quickly, wouldn't you? There is no point in delay."

There is no more in the kitty

This is the favorite ploy of buyers who do not want to be pestered by sales people. "Sorry, we have used up the budget." "We have overspent the project funds." "Our cash flow is perilous."

Don't fall for it. Probe the cash. Probe the budget. There is always, always, another budget somewhere which is not overspent. They can charge some of it into that, can't they? Find out when his new budget period starts. You can deliver then, can't you?

"You have got a lovely house," says Mr. Purchase, "but I must be honest with you. I cannot raise a high enough mortgage. I am just $2500 short. What can you do on the price?"

Why can't Mr. Purchase get a second mortgage, or sell his boat, or borrow the money from his brother? Why should you have to give him $2500?

They've got a goal. We've got five fouls and a penalty. On average we are winning

People can do funny things with figures. The quality is too low and the price is too high, so on average it seems about right. People are never going to quote you a figure which is not useful to *them*; the figure is always the best one they can select and it will be presented in the most favorable way for their case. So you can take it that every other figure they could produce is worse.

"I'll show you how low our electricity bills are," says Mr. Sells. Ask to see his gas bills and his central heating oil bills, too.

"I'm glad you have offered to pay my legal costs," says Mr. Sells. "But I gave you in exchange the quick deal that you wanted. You also wanted to move some things into the garage early, and I agreed to that. And I also undertook to have the bathroom window repaired at my cost and before you moved in. I'm doing three things for you, while you are doing only one for me. You are getting the best out of this deal."

It's only a little goal

Watch out when they break down the price into little chunks or use percentages.

"Would you be willing to take a small price reduction of, say, 2½%?—if I paid in cash?"

A reduction of 2½% does not sound like a lot, but on a $50,000 deal it is well over $1,000 to be paid out of someone's net profit.

"Taken over a year, the central heating will not cost you more than 10 cents an hour to run. That is just under $2,000 a year."

"If you buy our house, it is more expensive I agree, but if you keep it for ten years, then you will have all these marvelous extra amenities to enjoy all around you for only $1 per day. That is only 20 cents a day for each person in your family. Not only that, you will get all your money back and more when you come to sell the house, anyway." What is the extra cost? Over $3,500.

Can we have the option on the next goal?

Watch out for options; you might be tying yourself up to a deal which will be difficult to escape from.

"How much did you say you wanted for your house? Give me your best price," says Mr. Purchase. "If you decide to sell below that price, can I have the first option?"

Later Mr. Purchase is called by Mr. Sells, who tells him of an offer he has received and which he is willing to accept. "Thank you," said Mr. Purchase, "We will accept it at that price." Mr. Sells says that Mr. Purchase should better the offer, but receives the following reply. "No, you agreed that I should have the first option should you decide to sell below your original price. You are willing to sell at the new price you have quoted me. By the terms of our agreement together, you must do the deal with me at that price."

SUMMARY

Price is a very significant indicator of quality. Skilled buyers will generally concentrate the debate upon the pricing issue once they have identified the essential components of the deal. And they will give the strong impression that they will only buy for a low price. They will nearly always say this, but only sometimes will they really mean it. So the sales presenter should arouse their enthusiasm for the quality of the deal and should leave pricing arguments to the end.

A low price sales argument does not always win the day, because the buyer will need considerable reassurance about quality if he is to buy at low price. Where products and services are competing closely on quality, then price issues are narrow. But where there are wide variations in quality, or where the risk to the buyer of something going wrong is high, then price segmentation is wide.

Price arguments can often be turned through concentrating upon payment periods, or discounts or terms. It pays to get the other man to name his offer first wherever possible.

Profit benefits should be grossed up over periods of time ahead or over the whole volume of the deal. But cost arguments need to be spread thin or based upon a per unit comparison. It pays the buying negotiator to quote a lower price competitor; equally it pays the sales negotiator to compare his offering with one that is higher in price.

Don't pause after naming your price; go on to add a further benefit and finish with a question relating to some aspect of, say, delivery or after-sales service. Always ask for a quotation when buying—even if it is just to let them see that the price is on your mind. It will discourage them from loading the bill, or from playing "Buy now, bargain later."

∗   ∗   ∗

Now go back to the questionnaire at the start of this chapter and complete it again.

Demands, Concessions and Movement | 10

Fill in the answers to these questions first, then read the chapter. Fill in the answers again, and check your scores, from the end of the book.

Q.1 *You are an arbitrator in union and management disputes. A series of unofficial strikes has broken out over what seem to be petty grievances. Two unions are at loggerheads, and management is making noises about closing down the plant altogether. It threatens to turn into a major confrontation. What is your first objective, after you have understood the facts?*
(a) To tell the parties of your decision and leave them to implement it; (b) to get them to see the problem for themselves; (c) to equalize the bargaining power between the parties; (d) to narrow the areas of disagreement.

Score   **Score**

_____   _____

           Before reading chapter.   *After reading chapter.*

_____   _____

Q.2 *You are the promotion manager for your company, dealing with two travel agents in competition for your business. You have told them your price limit for your annual sales conference of 60 men booking in a Mexican hotel, but you want extra facilities included free of charge. You want three sightseeing trips, a free nightclub trip, two extra places in the plane and in the hotel for your directors, and so on. Without making any firm commitment on your part, do you:*
(a) ask them for your biggest demand first; (b) ask them for your smallest demand first; (c) tell them everything you want and let them sort it out; (d) it does not matter as long as you get it all across.

Score   **Score**

_____   _____

           Before reading chapter.   *After reading chapter.*

_____   _____

Q.3   *You are the travel agent competing for this bit of business. He is making his demands upon you. Do you:*
(a) agree to his first demand only if he gives you the order; (b) get all his requirements from him first; (c) give him a list of all your requirements; (d) tell him "no deal" on anything, and mean it?

Score   **Score**

_____   _____

Before reading chapter.   *After reading chapter.*

_____   _____

Q.4   *At Islip airport on Sunday you discover your chartered plane has engine trouble and is stuck in Nantucket. The manager of the operating company cannot tell you when the next plane will be available, but offers to put up your party overnight in a local hotel free of charge. He says you should be only a day or so late at the most. You notice that the booking regulations allow him a contractual escape route. What do you say to him?*
(a) Please have the plane fixed as quickly as possible. We understand how these things can happen when you fly; (b) we will sue you for the recovery of our costs, and for damages to our reputation; we will make life as difficult as possible for you, unless you solve this problem now; (c) it's a very serious situation and we shall have to think about our position; (d) give me your boss' home telephone number.

Score   **Score**

_____   _____

Before reading chapter.   *After reading chapter.*

_____   _____

Q.5   *You take a scheduled flight yourself, ahead of your party, just to check the local situation. But the arrangements there are in a mess. The travel agent's representative is not there. The hotel is overbooked and five of your people will have to stay elsewhere. The conference facilities are not complete with the necessary projectors and screens. The nightclub tour has not been booked. You have paid half the cash in advance, but the hotel has not received its share. Before they will let you even sign in, they want an undertaking in writing from you that they will be paid. Other hotels are full and no one else has a conference facility. Your party is airborne and on its way now. What do you do?*
(a) Concede immediately—if you don't, you may not have anywhere for your party to sleep; (b) open up the problem on both sides, appeal to their good nature, and give them your written assurance of payment; (c) tell them they

must look to the travel agent for their money, and show them that you have paid your side of the bill; (d) give them the payment guarantee only if they put right all the deficiencies in the facilities, including the nightclub tours.

Score   **Score**

_____   _____

Before reading chapter.   *After reading chapter.*

_____   _____

Q.6 *A telex from head office reveals that your travel agent has gone into liqui-dation. You will have to write off the money you have paid in advance. On reflection over the deal, you have not been very successful. You should have dealt with the other agent. What was the principal mistake you made?*
(a) Bargaining too hard; (b) failing to tie up the contractual details properly; (c) failing to double-check every stage of the process; (d) failure in the research and preparation stage.

Score   **Score**

_____   _____

Before reading chapter.   *After reading chapter.*

_____   _____

Demands, Concessions and Movement | 10

If one person is holding 200 people for ransom, it would be declared an illegal act in most countries. But if the location is New York City, the one person is managing agent for an apartment building, and the hostages are the 200 people living there, then the law will do little to help. The people have to help themselves.

Practically all the residents in this case had bought their apartments for their retirement. Apart from paying for their 99 year leases, the residents also had to pay a basic maintenance charge every year for services such as the elevators, cleaning, painting and repair of the exterior of the building, and for the resident porter. If the basic maintenance charge did not cover all the annual running costs completely, then the managing agents had the right to levy an "excess charge" upon each owner.

This technique you will note is called "Buy now—Bargain later" and is to be avoided if you are on the receiving end of it, and is to be encouraged if you are on the delivery end of it. The residents were squarely on the receiving end.

The managing agent's fee was paid out of the service charges levied upon the residents. The agent was supposed to look after the day-to-day problems such as damp walls, repairs to the fabric of the building, employment of the porter and the host of things needed to be done to maintain the services.

The problem for the residents was that the managing agents did not want to know of their difficulties. Queries were left unanswered. Replies were not given to letters. Little was done. Legal threats were largely ignored because the leases were drawn up in such a way as to make the building owners and agents legally liable for as little as possible.

This, you will notice, is a tactic called "Let's both play to these rules." So both the owners of the building and their managing agents were hard and experienced bargainers. It was easy for them to ignore the demands of the residents. Some residents suspected that the costs of the maintenance, which totalled well over $250,000 each year, were not controlled very well.

The power clearly rested with the managing agents. Under such a one-sided relationship, their demands were irresistible. Every time they demanded to be paid the excess charge, however much the residents complained, the residents had to pay up. Two residents were taken to court for non-payment, and the court found against them. The residents had to pay the legal costs of both sides, also. Whatever demands were made by the residents could be safely ignored by the agents—and their clients, the property owners, would not help either.

Before you can make demands on the other party, you have to be in a position of power. This means that the other party must either want something from you or can be made to suffer a problem. When the balance of power begins to be equalized, then demands and concessions begin to be exchanged. Whether the total deal takes only one minute to complete, or, as in the case of the residents, it takes three years, the process remains the same. Initially, at the approach stage, the parties are sizing each other up. They establish their power relationship together. Their opening "demands" are part of this power struggle. These opening demands are conceded to only by those in a very weak position (perhaps those who need the deal badly, or those who need it quickly) and by those who are inept at bargaining.

Hint for bargainers:

> *If experts concede your demands straight away, you*
> *should ask yourself "Why?" It is not normal.*

The serious exchange of demands and concessions takes place towards the end of the process. Usually, there is some moment when the process is stalled. Then something happens to obtain movement—one party makes a suggestion, which is taken up by the other.

Movement and closure can then follow very quickly. Almost in the same breath it seems, some deals can move from deadlock to completion. In other complex deals, the movement will be discontinuous, and the proceedings can be stalled several times.

Once movement is obtained, then the effect is similar to a social roller-coaster. There are many ups and downs, the process is rather thrilling, but disaster can always threaten.

The residents needed power. Divided they fell. Together in the form of a Residents' Association, they could exert pressure. Initially they could not agree among themselves, but they invited an outsider to chair the inaugural meeting. The association received an enormous filip, in the form of a huge increase in the excess service charges levied by the agent. Everyone wanted to join then.

The plays now moved as follows. The residents applied to have their association recognized legally by the court. That was resisted, but unsuccessfully, by the managing agents. The agents asked who were the paid-up members, but the information was refused to them.

The residents then found a legal flaw in the managing agent's work. They threatened to use it unless the agent discussed the problems with them. The agent ignored them.

The residents then hired a lawyer—not any lawyer, but a very tough one who specialized in handling landlord and tenant disputes in the slum areas of New York. This lawyer already had a very hard reputation.

The agents turned the matter to their own lawyer. Of course his charges would also have to be paid out of the general service charges on the building,

so here was a case of the residents paying for both the prosecution and defense
of their claims! Whether they won or lost, they would still have to pay.

Tip for bargainers:

> *Don't go to the law unless you have to.*
> *If you win, you'll lose. If you lose,*
> *you'll lose more. The only winners are*
> *the lawyers, expert witnesses,*
> *and judges.*

The residents knew they could not sustain a long fight. The costs could easily
go to $25,000 on appeal. They had raised a special fund that provided only
$500 for their legal expenses. They thought that the agent had guessed this,
and was using delay to break them. They had to bluff him out of this view.

They made their power play in three ways simultaneously. First they "leaked"
a rumor to one of the agent's employees that they had the backing of an
influential housing group which was going to use them as a test case. Money
would be no object. They then got a civic leader to say he would back their
case and raise the money from friends to "defend the old people's rights." This
story, with the leader's name and photograph, appeared in the press. They even
had some money donated to their cause through it. At the same time, they had
their own lawyer to back up their bluff by explaining to the other party's lawyer
that they were going to go all the way.

The agent broke, then, and agreed to a meeting. Someone always has to
break in the end—even if they walk out and the bargaining collapses, someone
has to make the decision. You cannot get movement without someone either
taking a risk and committing himself or by changing his mind. If both parties
stand firm, nothing will happen. You may have held out strongly to start with,
but there comes a moment when you will have to give. That can take a little
courage, because the other party might not come with you.

Tip for bargainers:

> *When you've got to go,*
> *you've got to go.*

Making demands

In making demands, it pays you to narrow down the areas of disagreement first.
That is, after the exploration stage, you should review the situation and identify
the areas where you both agree with each other. It's better if you do this review
yourself, rather than leaving it to the other party.

The review may have to be undertaken several times during the process, after
long and complex bargaining procedures have been completed. In this way, the
mountain of points outstanding at the start gradually reduces to the point where
both parties can see where the final settlement area remains.

If you are making demands, you should separate them and secure a broad
agreement to each one in turn *before* you make any committment yourself. You
should start with the most important one, secure their agreement to it, and

move to the next one without yourself having agreed to the overall deal. Here is one side of a conversation between a union negotiator facing a weak management.

"If you want the boys to stop the strike and to come back to work in time to get your big export order completed, then let us see what you are offering," says the union negotiator.

"My men won't begin to look at less than a 15% wage hike, you know that, so we can take that for granted. Now this productivity plan we have, which is causing so much trouble, it will have to be amended so that we all go back to a flat rate plan on top of the 15%, you agree to that?" (Yes.)

"The bonus on the overtime order itself. There is too much pressure on my men already. Some of them are working themselves into the ground. Their wives are kicking up a stink. We want a shift premium to be added to the normal overtime rates for this order. I take it that will be acceptable to you?" (Yes.)

"You have got to clear up this other aggravation, too, about the safety officer interfering with the way the boys are working. Those safety guards are very heavy to lift. The men have got backache. You will have to change the safety guards or change the safety officer. We don't mind which."

Hint for bargainers:

> *If their first demand is a big one then*
> *it pays to hold out for as long as possible.*
> *If you give in then, it should be only on the*
> *understanding that there will be no further*
> *demands.*

What the union man has done is to chip off the manager bit by bit. He has made no commitment himself at any stage. If the manager has fallen for it, then there is no reason why the union man can't actually end up by saying that he'll take the deal away to "the boys" to discuss it. Then he could come back with a few more demands. He also secured his important demand first. By not resisting the 15% claim, the manager left himself open to renewed pressure. If he had fought strongly, right at the start, so that both parties were exhausted by the time they secured agreement, then the union man would not have pressed so vigorously for the rest. Some of the demands he would have left until another day, particularly the demand relating to the safety guards on the machines.

Making concessions

The manager must make some concessions of course, otherwise he will have a resentful work force and a conflict bargaining situation on his hands. But he should make concessions slowly. He should make them separately. And he should start with small concessions.

The first rule is to let the other man open with a statement of what he wants. But find out all of what he wants, not just a bit of it. When you know it all, you are in a position to calculate the total cost.

Let him make the first big concession if you can. You may have to meet it with a counter-concession of your own to encourage him. But his concession to you should be big; your concession to him will be small.

Conserve your concessions. Work out concessions which do not cost you anything. This can be by supplying a reference, an introduction to a third party, an offer to help in some way, or by helping the other party with his timetable.

Question for bargainers:

*Why give it away, when you could
get something for it?*

As a buyer, your package for him will include several items, comprising money, payment time, terms, and conditions. Don't wrap all these up together in one package. Trade them, if you have to, bit by bit. Supposing your company pays its bills normally in thirty days. Don't give it away. Ask him for three months credit. He will fight you for it. Offer to pay him within thirty days, provided he gives you something in exchange, perhaps the 1½% extra discount you want. He will give it to you. What have you given him? Nothing that you would not give him anyway.

Try to get something big, for everything small you give. But keep the conversation loose and flexible, otherwise he will spot what you are up to and dig in his heels.

Keep a note of all your concessions to him. Re-state them often, because this will help to counter his later demands. "Look what we've given you so far," you say: "All the giving is on one side."

Also keep a note of all his concessions to you, but this is for recording purposes at the end of the meeting.

Obtaining movement

When the process is stalled the first party to move is at a disadvantage. So it can pay to make a trial movement first. This needs a signaling process along the lines of: "I will if you will."

You might try a hypothetical trade-off. "Look," you say, "You want this from us and we want that from you. Suppose we were to think again about our side of the issue, would you be prepared to do the same about yours?" What you have done is to link up two issues and suggest that there may be a trading position.

The person who offers a concession weakens his position. So if the other party suggests a link between two issues, then be careful. They may be trying to break through your position on a point where you are very powerful, while at the same time offering you something which you would probably get anyway.

When the managing agent met the residents' association committee and chairman face-to-face, the atmosphere was very hostile. No threats were offered by either side explicitly, but each party was very suspicious of the other. The agent offered to carry out some work, and to re-examine some of his working methods. He finally had to ask if the association would drop its legal action. The association knew it could not afford to go on with it, but the chairman was unwilling to give up this bargaining counter at this stage. The agent realized that he was not going to win this concession easily and so he made his own power play. Within three minutes the entire conflict was over. The agent had already modified his stand and had agreed to be more co-operative. But the association's position collapsed very quickly. They parted on a friendly basis and although it took another two years before the relationship was fully satisfactory to both parties, there was no doubt about the final outcome.

What the agent did was to explain that in the following year the service charges would have to be exceptionally high. Two boilers would need to be renewed; the outside fabric of the building would need repair; the five-yearly painting contract would be completed and each leaseholder would have to pay probably $1500 all in one year. "In the past, we have always managed to spread this cost over several years," said the agent, "but our lawyers tell us that we might be running afoul of the law. So we will have to put the whole cost on to your members in one year."

The association committee saw the danger immediately. Their members would be furious. They did a deal. The managing agent had successfully linked the issue of dropping the association's legal action with the threat of a very high service charge.

Another excellent method for obtaining movement out of a sticking situation is to ask for an adjournment, or to ask to refer the matter back to one's own side. Not enough use is made of the tactical recess in commercial negotiations. Everyone wants to do the deal in a hurry and in the open. It can be a bad mistake. Buy yourself time to think. Go out of the room and call your boss. It doesn't matter what you say to him: tell him it's a tactical call. When you go back you can get some movement, and also maintain your own credibility.

For example, when you said previously that it was out of the question for you to concede a particular point, your boss has now pointed out to you a way in which it can be done, as follows....

Advice for bargainers:

Always have a good reason for changing your mind. Never let them see you are playing.

Sometimes you can just get them to open up, if you do the same. You can appeal to their good nature, you can offer to come clean with what you really want, and so on. If you get the timing right, and you sense that they are trying to find a way to move as well, then the tactic will work. But if they are not interested, if they are still pressing hard, if there is not enough pressure on them to meet what you want, then don't use the tactic. They will simply use it to obtain your information and will not move with you.

There must be a mutual agreement to shift the position. This can be stated explicitly, or be sensed as an implicit understanding. What it means is that one party feels unable to hold to his position; but he must bring the other party with him if he can. The means of obtaining movement must be available to both parties.

Extra pressure at the right time may be necessary to get the other party moving. For example, you would have to be a masochist to enjoy working for this boss. He is president of a tire company with several large outlets. He is a wheeler-dealer who operates in an industry where wheeling-dealing is a total way of life. This man sets up all the price wars between dealers. In doing so, he does not make a lot of money, but he sells a lot of tires.

He telephoned his Indianapolis manager. "Joe, I have just done a very silly thing," he says. "You'll laugh when you hear it. Goodyear just gave me a really special offer on 50 large truck tires. It was a deal I couldn't refuse, the price was so cheap, only $1,800 each.

"The trouble is that we've now got to sell them," he went on. "How many can you take in Indianapolis?"

The Indianapolis manager exploded. "Listen, boss," he said, "I'm stuffed up to the eyeballs in truck tires, car tires, van tires, tractor tires. You keep on giving me more than the market can take. How can I sell these extra tires now?"

"O.K., Joe, O.K." said the boss. "I'm sorry, I quite understand. There's no problem. Look, just do me one personal favor, would you? Just take 16 of the Goodyear tires into your depot and do the best you can with them. If you have not sold them all in two weeks time, then give me a telephone call and tell me. I'll come over to you and sell them myself for you."

If you were his Indianapolis manager, wouldn't you move them?

Tactics to give little away

Listen carefully to all that he says, treat him nicely, provide the best explanation of your case and prove it where you can.

Let him do all the checking, do not offer to do it for him. Wear him down. "Before my company can even begin to consider these price increases you are suggesting," you might say, "you will have to give us a breakdown. Show us the justification for your arguments, then we will see."

Three weeks later, after a lot of work, he returns to you with the figures. "No," you say, "that's not the way my company needs to see the figures; you will have to allocate the costs differently,"—and so on, until in the end he will settle for two-thirds of what he wanted originally, with relief at not having to do any more work.

Of course, the problem will recur, and on the next occasion he will be firmer in his demands. Your action in wearing him down has warned him that you are a difficult person with whom to deal. So he will hold out more firmly next time. Perhaps on the next occasion you can deal with him differently. You might on this subsequent occasion be able to promise him in the future, new business for him perhaps, provided that he modifies his demand for price increases.

Tell him that everyone is treated equally, and give him third party references of this to prove what you say.

Breaking deadlock

If the bargaining process is stuck solid, then different tactics must be used. You might get the process going by taking it in very small bites, and taking very simple issues. You might break the deadlock by changing the time scale. If both parties are thinking of the short-term benefits and obligations, then you might move to discuss the long-term issues. By securing agreement on the aims for the long term, it is often possible to show that short-term objections are relatively minor and this will help to free the situation.

You will need flexibility here. You will need to be able to suggest a new type of deal constructed in a totally different way, and you will need to float new ideas.

You might have to hold out hard for a deal which you know he will refuse. Then you can suggest the deal you wanted in the first place, as a compromise.

Finally, you can bring in a different bargainer. A new man will often get movement where the old and familiar face has failed, simply because he is unknown, he thinks in a different way, and he can suggest new moves. He brings a feeling of excitement to a stale situation, and this is his principal advantage.

TACTICS AND PLAYS

Our manager says we must not play like that

When the other party is defending against your pressure, he can fall back on his rule book, or his company policy, or on established precedent, or his instructions, or his limited authority. It is then difficult for you to insist, without causing deadlock. In a position of strength, it always pays to put in a bargainer who is given little discretion. He will then fall back on his instructions. He cannot move, he tells you, until he receives different instructions. If you are making a weak demand at the time, then you will let it go.

"I'm sorry," said Mr. Agent. "We shall be glad to handle your house sale for you—we already have someone who is interested—but I am afraid our company policy is that we must have sole rights for the first six weeks. It applies to everyone, this rule."

That's not part of the game

Sometimes it pays for a negotiator to underline a particular demand or set of demands by saying that they are "non-negotiable." It is a handy device to use early on in the process, in order to anticipate pressure on these points by the other party. Usually, such a phrase means exactly what it says. It is a closing phrase. It is extremely difficult for a bargainer to maintain his credibility if he backs down on this statement. It must be said firmly, and clearly, without equivocation. Then the other party will believe it.

The counter to the phrase is to ignore it. Change the subject, come back to it later. Pretend you have not heard it. There are a dozen ways of cutting the deal so that you can still get what you want by slipping around his policy. In the end, you can ask him to find ways of getting around his own sticking point. If you have him on the hook, then he will wriggle around his policy somehow. In the long run, everything is negotiable if they want the deal badly enough.

Let's have half-time now

Very few people ever refuse to let the other party have a quiet talk in private amongst themselves. Asking for a recess is a good way of buying time to think. But if you are going to use the device to try to obtain movement, then you must first make certain that the other party is willing to move from their position if you are willing to move from yours.

Otherwise you will return from the adjournment offering your concession, to find the other party has strengthened its resolve. Before you break, you must ensure that both parties are committed to moving on the resumption.

"We are not getting anywhere like this," says Mr. Purchase. "My survey of your house shows that $500 worth of work needs to be done. You refuse to pay for this, you also refuse to produce your own survey. I want you to pay for it all. Why don't we have a break for a while? Do I take it that you are willing to move a little on your side on this issue, if I move a little on my side? Shall we think about that, and each come up with our proposals for solving this deadlock?"

Showing dissent

This is a favorite play where more than one person is involved in a bargaining team. An argument breaks out between the two partners, over whether a concession should be made or not. It is conducted in front of the opposing team and is designed entirely for their benefit. (This is quite different from where genuine argument breaks out in one team. In this case, the team should fight it out behind closed doors, preferably in a sound-proofed room—padded, as well.)

"Henry, you know we can't pay anything towards the cost of the repairs called for in his survey, because we are up to the limit on our money," says Mrs. Sells.

"But it seems only fair to go a little way to help him," says Mr. Sells.

"Well, I don't want to sell the house anyway. I would prefer you to take it off the market, quite frankly. Look at all the moving costs we've got. It's up to you," says Mrs. Sells. Mrs. Sells, as you can see, is a very tough lady. She is strengthening Mr. Sells' hand. When the parties now go away to think about it, Mr. Sells will only have to concede a little towards the survey costs, perhaps one-third. Otherwise he might have ended up paying for half of the costs. The tactic has saved him perhaps $750.

Let's both kick the same way

You can always tell a professional negotiator by the way he secures agreements on small issues first. "Let us see where we agree with each other," he says. His

conversation is littered with phrases and questions such as: "I take it you agree…"
and "I assume," and "You will have no objection."

But be careful and listen hard. In this list of agreed matters, he can sneak in
one or two items to which you would not agree, or he can phrase remarks in
such a way as to enable him to cry "Foul" if you later reject them. "Oh, but
did we not agree to that early on?" he will ask, in mock horror. If you are going
to kick the ball the same way as he, then be careful you don't kick it into your
own goal.

"Even if we can't agree on the price," says Mr. Purchase, "let us see where
we can agree. You want to sell, we want to buy. We are both agreed about not
using an estate agent. We both want to complete the deal quickly, and we both
agree on the results of the survey. Now, how far are we really apart on price?"

Be careful. Who said that you wanted to complete the deal quickly? You
have got all the time in the world, haven't you? If he wants to complete quickly,
that's his problem. Of course, you might be able to accommodate him, but not
if it means you lose out on your price….

Faking a run

Be careful that they are not faking a run, by making you an offer that they know
you will refuse. Afterwards they sit pat, until you come up with an alternative.
Or they may suggest a new deal—this is the one they wanted in the first place,
but you would not have accepted it originally.

"The house needs $5,000 worth of work," says Mr. Purchase, "for repairs
and painting, plus $2,500 for rot proofing. There is another $7,000 to be spent
on clearing the garden and other outside work on the garage and drive, and if
we can't complete the contract for three months, that will cost me an extra
$2,500 in bridging loan interest. That is a total of $17,000. If you knock $17,000
off this price of yours, then we shall have a deal, and we shall get all the work
done ourselves."

"No, no," you reply, "I cannot agree to that." Then they go quiet, waiting
for you to suggest something. You will concede something, if they wait long
enough.

The counter to it is to make a dummy run of your own. "That would not
leave me enough money," you say. "I can move quickly and let you in. I'll get
a couple of guys to work with me on the garden, the rot proofing, the painting
and repairs, which will take a couple of days to complete. I'll knock $1,200 off
the price if you pay for my lawyer's costs, my estate agent's bill, and pay me
$1,500 towards the loan I'll need if I move early, and we'll call it quits. How
does that suit you? Oh, and I will only charge you an extra $2,500 for the
fixtures and fittings; they are worth $6000 really." Now it is your turn to sit
pat, and wait for him.

Somewhere in the middle, you probably have a deal going.

SUMMARY

Isolate the points of disagreement between the two parties. Identify the most important demand you want and name this first. Secure their commitment to it, without making any commitment yourself, and then move to the next most important. At some point they will catch on to your game and will resist future demands, but meanwhile you will have obtained most of what you want. Do not be too eager to close the deal before he is ready too. Your excitement will allow room for the other party to put in demands of his own.

Trade concessions for concessions. Store them up. Do not give things away without getting something in return even if it is part of your normal package. If they want something badly, then hold back a bit on it. You will secure something in exchange.

If you are deadlocked, then make sure that they will agree to move with you if you can find a way to move. Otherwise you will find yourself moving to a new position just to keep the discussion open. Now they can use your new position as a starting point, and they will sit tight.

Real deadlock needs an unemotional approach to break it. Take small issues first which can be agreed, then move to larger points of disagreement. Do not gameplay when trying to get things moving again.

Conflict Bargaining and Disputes | 11

Answer these questions before reading the chapter. After reading the chapter, answer the questions again. Then score both sets of answers.

Q.1   *Your company is heading for the rocks. You can head off disaster by shutting down part of a factory, laying off 250 people, or by withdrawing from a productivity agreement which is working against you, or by fudging some of the figures so that bonus rates are not so high. What do you do?*

(a) *Open up with the unions on your options;* (b) *fudge the figures;* (c) *re-negotiate the productivity agreement;* (d) *shut the factory.*

Score   **Score**
___   ___

Before reading chapter.   *After reading chapter.*

___   ___

Q.2   *As the company accountant, what is your policy towards creditors, and the checking of suppliers' invoices?*

(a) *You check invoices and query all mistakes, whether in your favor or not;* (b) *you check all invoices, but only query mistakes when they are against you. Suppliers' errors in your favor you leave;* (c) *you do not check invoices and pay according to the terms agreed;* (d) *you take every possible advantage you can from the suppliers, all mistakes in your favor, all settlement discounts, all the credit they will let you have.*

Score   **Score**
___   ___

Before reading chapter.   *After reading chapter.*

___   ___

Q.3   *This could be the start of an important business relationship. You are preparing the final draft of the agreement. Your boss wants you to exclude one item you have promised to provide to the other party. It is not big, but he* *says it might set a precedent for the future. Actually, you don't think they will even notice the omission. The agreement was hard to close and you do not want to open it up again. Do you:*

(a) *forget it and see if they pick it up;* (b) *come clean with them and try to re-negotiate;* (c) *persuade your boss that you are committed to your word;* (d) *let him tell the other party about it?*

Score   **Score**

_____   _____

Before reading chapter.   *After reading chapter.*

_____   _____

Q.4   *For years you and your fellow workers have held this waste disposal company at ransom. The work consists of transporting nuclear waste in lead containers to dockyards where it is shipped out to sea and dumped. Every time it comes to wage bargaining you and your colleagues in other similar plants threaten to strike. The effect could be horrendous if radioactive waste piled up. Management is always terrified that the newspapers will get the story and always caves into your power. You always make a high demand, then climb down. Management always makes a low offer, then you force them up. A new owner takes over the company; for the first time they show you their draft accounts. Clearly they are in trouble. The president looks you in the eye and says: "This is our first offer. And it is also our last offer. If you close us down, then you close us down. But if we go on the way we have been going on, then we will be closed down through our losses. It is up to you."*

(a) *Do you accept his offer?* (b) *do you call the boys out on strike?* (c) *do you stall a bit and make threatening gestures?* (d) *do you seek a productivity agreement?*

Score   **Score**

_____   _____

Before reading chapter.   *After reading chapter.*

_____   _____

Q.5   *As airline manager, you find that fog is delaying your flights. Your passengers are arriving and missing their connections. Everything is chaotic. Your assistant is tugging your arm, an important telephone call is waiting for you, you are being paged over the loudspeaker, and your personal bleeper is sounding. A woman, puce with anger, confronts you amid the crowd and screams that your airline has lost her suitcase, she has to attend her son's wedding next day, and she is clad in jeans and T-shirt only. What do you do?*

(a) *Pass her immediately to your assistant;* (b) *offer her a drink in the airline lounge;* (c) *tell her you are very busy as she can see, ask her to wait;* (d) *tell her she will receive compensation;* (e) *ask her to repeat her story to you.*

Score   **Score**

_____   _____

       Before reading chapter.   *After reading chapter.*

_____   _____

Q.6   *You are a dentist in private practice. This patient owes you a considerable sum of money and his account is well overdue. When will you raise the topic with him?*

   (a) *You won't. You know he is good for the money and it is unprofessional;* (b) *you will mention it casually as you are drilling his teeth;* (c) *before doing the work;* (d) *afterwards, your receptionist will mention it to him.*

Score   **Score**

_____   _____

       Before reading chapter.   *After reading chapter.*

_____   _____

Q.7   *You are contracted to supply stage settings to a film producer. But they have made life very difficult for you, through changing their minds, adding on all sorts of new things, making excessive demands for speedy work. And they forced the price of the contract down to the bone. What should you do? The work is already unprofitable and the film is not finished yet.*

   (a) *Immediately make a record of every single alteration to the contract, every extra cost, and tell the producer about it at once;* (b) *wait until you know the full extent of the costs, then submit the bill in the normal way. You have a legal right to charge for all the extras;* (c) *"load" the bill with all kinds of costs, in the knowledge that you will have to negotiate a settlement;* (d) *threaten to pull out of the contract unless they agree to pay for the costs to date, and re-negotiate the remainder of the deal. They cannot do without you.*

Score   **Score**

_____   _____

       Before reading chapter.   *After reading chapter.*

_____   _____

Q.8   *A tire manufacturer has stolen your retail tire business from you. They encouraged you to overtrade, to stock up heavily using extended credit from them, then they called their money in when the market took a down-turn. It is a question of selling-out to them or going bust. They have offered you a job with them. What will you do?*

(a) Accept the job and learn all you can before setting out on your own again; (b) accept the job but secretly nurse revenge; (c) go bust and to the devil with them; (d) sell-out and go your own way; (e) fight them with every weapon you can, sell off the stock cheaply, tell your suppliers and bankers what is going on and ask them to hold off demands for payment, raise complaints about the supplier, fight them in court and lose if you have to, but go down fighting all the way.

Score   **Score**
_____   _____

        Before reading chapter.   *After reading chapter.*

_____   _____

Q.9   *For years your labor relations have been wracked with disputes, inter-union squabbles, poor output, high costs and sour morale everywhere. You are the new boss. How do you approach this problem?*

(a) Tell everyone the facts of life, and show who is boss; (b) take each issue piecemeal as it comes along; (c) persuade the workers of the benefits of productivity bargaining; (d) re-organize the existing management and ask for co-operation; (e) bring in a new management team loyal to you; (f) behave normally, but use every opportunity to show that you mean exactly what you say, no more, and no less. You leave yourself no bargaining room.

Score   **Score**
_____   _____

        Before reading chapter.   *After reading chapter.*

_____   _____

Conflict Bargaining and Disputes | 11

All deals contain the seeds of conflict. As the two parties move together, the options for both of them begin to be closed off. They become more and more committed to one another. In the end, they become locked-in, so that neither party can easily escape from its commitments. At this point, conflict can occur.

Conflict bargaining is commonly violent and usually dirty. If one party gains something, the other sees it as a loss to them. It is therefore competitive. It sours industrial relations, it litters the world's courtrooms, it damages the social, political, and economic order. The world's history consists for the most part of the tales of disputes, fights and wars. Clearly conflict bargaining is a bad thing. But equally clearly, it is here to stay.

In November 1977, a diminutive South African was appointed to sort out one of the most sordid of the world's industrial relations problems. Few people had heard of him previously, except for some astute investors who held shares in an old-established British company making chloride batteries, whose fortunes had been revitalized in the previous ten years by Sir Michael Edwardes.

Few commentators held out any hope for the future of British Leyland at the time. Indeed, as this is written, there is no certainty of the company's survival even now.

British Leyland is a classic example of how people get into conflict situations, even though their best interests are served by collaborative bargaining.

British Leyland was a mish-mash of different car manufacturing companies which had been thrown together with a strong push from the government of the day. The idea was that only one very large company could compete in world markets with the giants of the industry, be they American or Japanese. As different companies, these outfits had varying management qualities, but at least each of them had a corporate spirit and a tradition of its own. But when all were together, this spirit did not exist.

With the sweeping changes made in organization structure, the in-fighting began. Each unit in the company aimed for its own self-interest. Deals were reneged upon—by groups of workers, by union representatives and by managements also. The entire company became the scene of industrial guerilla war. Worker fighting worker, factory fighting factory, management fighting management, rapacious greed everywhere was fuelled by fear and disillusion.

In short, no one could trust anyone else. And that is the cause of conflict bargaining. The conflict starts by one party not delivering some part of its side of the bargain to the other, *in the eyes of the other party*. There may exist genuine misunderstanding between the parties over what has been agreed. Or one party may have squeezed the other party too hard, or used too much leverage, or used threatening behavior. Under such circumstances, their opposite numbers become suspicious and apprehensive of their motives and tactics.

When that happens, then conflict becomes a probability, not just a possibility.

Conflict nearly always starts for the first time towards the end of the bargaining process. Before then, both parties have too many alternatives, and each party takes pains to hold the other to the bargaining table. The simplest, most profitable, and pleasantest way of doing this is by exchanging mutual benefits.

But towards the end, almost anything can trigger off a conflict. Commonly one party becomes fearful of some aggressive action by the other, at a point when they themselves are weak. The other party might threaten them for example: "Look, if you do not complete this deal on these terms before Wednesday of next week, then we shall have to pull out altogether." Such a crude statement of pressure and power is likely to cause the other party to re-examine the entire process of bargaining so far. They find other instances of pressure which sow further seeds of doubt in their minds. They feel they are being taken for a ride. The mutual trust the bargaining parties have built up together is destroyed. A counterattack is launched. "All right," they say, "if that's the way you want to play it, then go ahead and pull out. If you do we shall sue you for the recovery of our costs, plus damages because we have lost other opportunities through dealing with you. And, in addition, we now renounce all concessions made to you so far, and we shall go back to the terms of business we were proposing originally."

Hint for strong bargainers:

> *Never boast about your power. It makes the*
> *other man afraid, and that makes for bad deals.*

Now the parties are seriously in conflict. Instead of the mutual embrace of goodwill, one party has thrown a punch at the other. They have forgotten that one outstanding characteristic of human beings is the ability to counter punch. Even when he is going to lose the fight, a man will still go down punching.

If the two parties are locked-in so that they must continue to deal with each other in the future, then conflict of this kind becomes built into the structure of the relationship. If one party finds subsequently that the other party cannot be trusted, then on the next round of bargaining they themselves become firmer in their demands. They will use their power more obviously. And if they feel hurt, they will also seek revenge. And so it goes on, until subsequently the conflict is introduced *before* bargaining starts by open displays of power (strikes, etc.) and threat signals (lawyers' letters, etc.). Conflict is now rooted in the relationship.

How, then, did Sir Michael Edwardes bring about such a change in British Leyland that in 1980 disputes are minimal, factories have been closed, lay-offs on a massive scale have been accepted, the movement of plant from one site to another has been completed ahead of schedule, working practices have been reformed, many demarcation rules between skilled workers have been abandoned, and a wage increase of between 5% and 10% has been accepted at a time when the average increases for all workers in the country were 20%? The situation is far from perfect—it will never be that. But it is unbelievably better than it was.

The way in which the changes were brought about is an object lesson in handling conflict disputes. You must ensure that the other man knows, for an absolute certainty, that you mean what you say. And he must know the impact of this upon himself. And he must see that there is a collaborative means of securing his own best interests through your help. Never allow him to hope that he can get more by playing rough. Even if it costs you an arm and a leg, even though the deal is hopelessly uneconomic for you—this is the price you must pay if you want collaboration.

Hint for conflict bargainers:

> *Never threaten explicitly unless you mean it.*
> *And remember you may have to go through with it.*

The first essential step is to establish your credibility. Sir Michael Edwardes has the reputation of being straight with everyone. He states neither more nor less than the truth to his own Board, to the workers, to his management, to his customers and suppliers.

The second essential step is to deal with the problem head-on. In British Leyland's case, this was reputedly the seven week unofficial strike at the Bathgate truck and tractor plant in Scotland in the autumn of 1978. Some 1,500 engineering machinists were told that the company would close the plant and a £32 million capital injection would be wiped out. The men went back to work with nothing.

It was not the first test, nor will it be the last, before total credibility has been restored on the management side. But now the BL workers know the facts about the company's situation. Communications with the workforce have been improved.

The workforce also realizes that when circumstances improve in the company and in the industry as a whole, they will be the first to benefit. The sole alternative is unemployment for them. The same is true for management.

Lastly, in the bargaining process, the BL management's first offer tends to be its last. They leave themselves very little room for maneuver, and this is obvious to the other party. This factor minimizes the game play.

Handling disputes

The simplest form of conflict bargaining in normal commercial practice is handling complaints. The man with a grievance, whether it is justified or not, is usually in an emotional state. Some can be wild with anger. Just watch an airport lounge when flights are disrupted. The atmosphere is charged with tension, movement is unstable. For the most part people keep their temper, but from time to time disputes will break out. These will usually be launched by passengers who have just turned up and have suddenly realized that their expected journey is not going to take place. This is the most difficult moment. After they have gotten used to the idea, they settle down, but care is always needed to reassure them that everything which can be done is being done.

So the use of delay is an important tactic in handling disputes, because it provides time for the emotions to be drained. But be careful, because delay usually helps one party to become stronger than the other.

The first principle if you are on the receiving end is to defuse their emotion. Hear out their grievance fully. Ask them to tell you the full story. Take it seriously (however frivolous you think it to be). If they are still emotional when they tell you the story, then get them to repeat it over and over again until they take breath and tell you quietly and sanely. You have no alternative for dealing with an emotionally disturbed complainant other than to let him get it all out. On no account do anything to disturb him further, such as by arguing with him, rebutting directly his criticism, counter-attacking, or laughing at him. Offer to look into it, but offer no other concessions initially except sympathy with him that he should experience this problem. If he attacks you, or your organization, turn the other cheek. He is in the wrong, and this is to your advantage. By retaliation, you will put yourself in the wrong. Then, later, he can cry "Foul" and the situation will look bad for you.

Tip for bargainers handling disputes:

> *Don't let them catch you*
> *breaking the rules.*

So, initially, be serious and submissive if their anger is genuine. Later you can exert more obvious control.

In handling disputes and conflict situations, it is necessary to assess the power relationship. This in turn is usually dependent upon the official or unofficial rules which are guiding both parties.

Examine the legal framework carefully. Look at *your* rights in law, both from your point of view, and also how your rights look from his point of view. Can he interpret the rules in his favor? If you were his legal adviser, what would you say to him and how would you approach the subject? Examine *his* rights in law carefully, again from your perspective and also from his.

But the legal framework forms only the background to the dispute. It is not everything.

A service company put up a proposal to a company selling wines, for a distribution project. Their terms of business stated that acceptance could be by word of mouth or in writing. In the event of late cancellation of the project after acceptance, then the costs of the service would be repayable in full, by the wine distributors. The dealings were with the distribution manager who agreed to the proposal and settled the dates for the start of the project. This decision was minuted, but a peculiar form of phrasing was used.

Later the distribution manager put in his resignation to his company, which was in financial trouble, and the production director cancelled the project on the grounds that he himself had not approved of it, nor would he have approved of it if he had known. The service organization claimed the payment of the full project fee, and their management was very angry at the cancellation.

In practice, they were in some difficulty in law. The contract could and would be disputed. So other means had to be found to make the company pay. The service organization realized they could not get their full charge back, but they formulated the highest claim they could, and backed it with figures. They held the dispute to the production director personally, sensing that he was himself in some personal difficulty over the matter.

If the legal framework to the dispute is not to the bargainer's advantage, then other levers can be used. The bargainer is severely constrained however if he wants to go on doing business with the other party. The other party may gently use its commercial power of the future relationship to force the settlement of a particular issue. "If you want more business from us, you'll have to drop all these claims," is the usual response. The counter to this—not always successful—is to take the bargaining out of the hands of the person who is responsible for the normal business relationship, giving him no discretion at all over the matter, so that he can refuse to let the issue of future business be linked together with the dispute. Someone else, preferably a third party, or an arbitrator, someone divorced from the usual relationship, should then take up the running on the dispute. It can help to send the original bargainer away on something like an extended overseas visit, otherwise the other party may attempt to use him to help their arguments.

It was clear that the wine company production director was very skillful with the words he used in letters, and it was clear that he was going to drag out the dispute if he could. By dragging it out for a long time, the supplier would give up in the end and settle for a small figure. The production director was claiming that his distribution manager had not agreed to the project. He set up meetings with the service company to discuss the dispute and then cancelled them.

So the service company let the matter go until the distribution manager had left the wine company. They figured that this would weaken the production director's position. Then they went in hard with their threats. They threatened legal action, they said they would take the dispute above the production director's head to the chairman of his parent group company, they threatened to involve the Wine and Spirit Trade Association, and in general to cause as much damage as they possibly could.

Then they did something else which was to turn the key to the issue. Having put the maximum amount of pressure on the production director personally, they had one of their staff call up the ex-distribution manager at his new place of employment. He was told that the service company was so angry about the dispute that they would proceed with the action as a matter of principle, notwithstanding the economic consequences to themselves. They would inflict the maximum possible damage upon the production director personally. They gave the distribution manager an "unofficial" idea of the settlement figure they would go for. They did not mind if he passed on this information to the production director, his ex-boss. Within twenty-four hours the dispute was over, and a settlement was agreed.

Bargainers:

Never tell him you are going to punch him in the eye.
But you can get someone else to tell him.

In handling disputes, it is necessary to examine the power structure between the parties, and to see how this power can be built up. It is no use threatening if the other party sees you have not the power to carry out your threat. In practice, explicit threats are not usually so fearful a prospect as an implied threat of some indeterminate action.

In handling disputes, it is vital to put the case together quickly, before the issue fades from your people's memory. Who said what, and to whom, is very important and should be recorded on paper as soon as the dispute breaks out. Many, many disputes have been lost when they should have been won, simply because one party was uncertain of its own case.

A printing company was accused of doing poor work by a customer who refused to pay. So the printer threatened to sue. The customer maintained rather poor records, while the printer maintained excellent records. The printer put his facts and figures together immediately in a concise document, and made the personnel concerned sign formal statements about their view of the dispute.

The customer used stalling tactics. He sent a check for half the amount in "full and final settlement." This was returned to him, with a counter claim for damages and interest on the overdue account. When the issue looked like it was going to court, the customer found his case was hopeless because no one could really remember in detail what had happened. They could not brief their own lawyer properly and he advised abandonment of the claim. They settled the account and paid the costs of both parties.

Here is a four-step guide to the handling of disputes.

1. Quickly gather the records together and the details of conversations, minutes of meetings. Ensure that your people make formal statements about what happened, which they should sign. Establish immediately the facts and figures, assess the costs to you, the costs to them. Calculate how much you might lose through the dispute and calculate how much they might lose.

2. Calculate your bargaining power, both in the short term and in the long term. If you are in a weak position, then you may have to take some action to build your power before the bargaining starts. Make an assessment of whether time is going to work in your favor or in theirs.

3. Present your case to them in a factual way without revealing all your hand. If you are strong, then distance yourself from them by writing to them. If you are weak, then you will need to become closer to them. See them face-to-face. If you are weak, then do not threaten. You will need to pull them through with persuasion.

4. Keep a cool head. Even in the face of strong pressure and personal attacks

made upon you, don't lose your cool. Even when their arguments are totally unjustified, reply calmly and carefully.

Tip for bargainers:

Don't get into disputes. Be honest, deliver
more than you promise, explain the difficulties
to them, and deal only with nice people.

The principal factor is power, however, as in all bargaining situations. Remember that power can be built up in a number of ways. It can pay you to work on one man and on his personal feelings. It also pays to try the nice way of persuasion first, and then to display your power if the nasty way is the only way that will work.

Few customers win disputes with garages. If you threaten not to pay them they will not release the car. Once they have your money, then they are not bothered about your complaint. They become very unwilling to admit liability for anything because this could lead to a default on their insurance policy or a third party claim for large damages.

A little Japanese car was taken in for a routine service, and to have the brakes repaired. The bill was excessive, but the garage said that a great deal of work had been necessary and the customer paid up reluctantly. He felt that he should have been told in advance of the high cost of the repairs. Two days and 200 miles later the brakes failed on the car. The garage would not admit liability nor would they take it back into their workrooms.

It would have been difficult for the customer to prove in law that the garage had been negligent, and it would have been expensive to try. But, on paper, the situation did look bad for the garage.

So the customer built his power another way. He was an executive in a public relations agency and he wrote a press release on his own personal letterhead which factually described the history of the incident. It did so in such a way as to make it look bad for the garage yet without being open to a libel suit. The press release stuck absolutely to the facts. At the foot of the press release, he put a distribution list which included all the local papers, radio and television stations, the motoring trade magazines, etc. He dated the press release for three days ahead.

This press release was sent to the manager of the garage which had handled the service, with a letter which explained that it was going to be distributed in three days time without fail. The author of the letter could not be contacted by telephone in that period. If the facts were disputed, then the car could be found for inspection at such and such an address.

A copy of the press release and the covering letter was also sent to the service director and the sales director of the car manufacturer. Immediately they pressured the garage to take care of the problem. Within ten hours the car had been collected, repaired, washed and cleaned inside and out and returned to the owner.

Further tip for bargainers:

If you've got to play rough, then play very rough.

Productivity bargaining

To any business manager, the idea of productivity bargaining makes such good sense that he genuinely feels the workers are stupid if they do not accept it. When he cannot understand their position, he often suspects some malevolent motive behind their refusal to co-operate fully. After all, argues the manager, if labor agrees to scrap old work habits and wasteful practices in order to increase the efficiency of the company, then management will return some of the gains to the labor force. What could make better sense than that? Labor argues that by introducing more automation, the total number of people employed will go down. Yes, replies the manager, but those who remain will be more wealthy and we can look after the problem of unemployment gradually by not taking on workers when people leave.

But the essence of the labor force hostility to productivity bargaining is much deeper than this model shows. First, there is a traditional suspicion that management does not always play fair when it comes to sharing out the gains. These, it seems, have to be fought for again and again. Secondly, if management is allowed an inch it will take a mile—a precedent established in one part of the production operation is then used as a lever in another. (Management, of course, accuses labor of this as well.)

There is also a very fundamental problem of world underemployment which lies at the heart of the argument. The world is gradually, bit by bit, running out of its resources of material wealth. It has an abundance of labor. Technology is facing an impossible race with the increase in the world population. Technology is often designed to take the labor out of the process—at the very time when the world needs more jobs.

Job creation is a very real world problem, not just a British or American problem. It applies as much to a factory in Peking or Moscow as it does in Newcastle or New Jersey. Just take a look around any Russian factory to see the numbers of people not doing anything. They cannot be fired; there is no unemployment benefit in the Russian system. Everyone must have a job. But technology and the inevitable slowdown of the world's economic growth rate are taking huge numbers of people out of work.

Obvious truth for productivity bargainers:

People can be unemployed as easily
in work as out of it.

Not only is the workers' representative uneasy about creating further unemployment, there is another emotional barrier which gets in the way. It is this. Managers in general have nice jobs. They have power, they get involved in decisions, they have privileges that are not available to workers. Workers, in general, have rotten jobs by comparison. Why should workers co-operate with managers? Their instincts are against it.

This section on productivity bargaining has been included in the chapter on Conflict because the principles and procedures are similar. Suspicion about each party's motives and doubt about the facts will abound. Reassurance and trust are needed on both sides. Once agreement is reached, then both parties must deliver in full their side of the bargain. When a productivity agreement is used by one party to escape from its other commitments, then this will sour the relationship for a long time.

Question for the managers of workers:

If you've got all the power and all the glory,
why should they help you get more?

Therefore both parties need to be absolutely clear about the measurements. The rules and conditions must be laid down with precision and agreed by both sides. Productivity agreements involve change. Human beings do not like change much—and out of change some people do well, but others do badly. So the union negotiators have a difficult task to deliver their own side of any bargain.

First, it is necessary to establish on both sides that a productivity deal is desirable. It is useless for only one party to go for it, because they can be taken apart subsequently by the other party who will easily fudge the agreement in some way. Or they will cry "Foul" at some minor transgression of the agreement by the other party and use this as a lever to withdraw their co-operation.

Secondly, it is necessary to look at the effect the deal will have on other groups of people, other managements in other locations. Through a productivity agreement at one site, we may be offering a lever to others, who will make demands upon us.

Can each party deliver its side? Can the work be measured and assessed accurately? Are there rivalries between different groups on either side? What is the downside-risk—what will happen if things do not go as well as anticipated— do the people involved share in the losses as well as in the gains?

Is a phased implementation necessary, and are there adequate procedures for consultation in the event of special problems occurring? Is there a monitoring system and a procedure for regular review of the working of the agreement? Is there a provision for renegotiating the agreement if this becomes necessary?

The lines of communication must be clearly established, and both parties to the agreement must work together to make it stick.

Clearly, a very high degree of trust is required by both parties. The best productivity deals take a long time to negotiate, and both parties take great care to behave in an impeccable manner. Problems must be reported immediately to the other party and the unofficial lines of communication kept open.

Productivity bargaining is not the arena of competition. It cannot withstand bargaining game play. It cannot hold against threatening behavior or any other action which can be associated with coercion. It is one of the highest forms of team bargaining process which can be devised.

Going to the courthouse door

The old and worn-out tactic of threatening to take the other party to court to settle a dispute is played badly most of the time.

Usually it is a tired way of putting a dispute which is troublesome into the hands of a lawyer, to let him sort it out. He earns his living from such disputes. If you were a lawyer, would you want to settle disputes quickly or slowly, remembering that you will be paid for the amount of work you do?

Most disputes left to lawyers are settled out of court at some compromise point. One party or the other is usually more experienced at handling such affairs, and they get the better of such deals.

Here is a guide for handling legal disputes. First, know the law yourself, enough to argue your side convincingly so that the other party gets the strong impression that you yourself know what you are talking about.

Build up the strength of your case, and display the strength of your bargaining position. Show them your power to embarrass them, but stay absolutely within the law—otherwise they will call "Foul" and defeat you in court. Get the facts established quickly. Get them right. Make your own side sign statements about what happened. Anything you write to them should help you if it is read out in court. Face-to-face you can say what you like so long as the other party has no witness to the conversation.

Offer them a deal which is difficult to refuse. For example, if you want to offer a deal to settle their account, mark your letter "Without Prejudice" and send it with a check for part payment in "full and final settlement" of the account. Tell them in your letter that if they wish to accept this offer, then all they have to do is to bank your check. If they wish to reject it, then they must return the check to you. The other party will usually collapse at this stage and take the part payment, particularly if you spell out the costs to them of not taking it.

Point up the legal deficiencies in their case. Scorn their briefing to their lawyer. (All lawyers worry that their litigious clients have not told them the full and proper story.) Don't show your own hand. But explain that in court you will wish to see specific data to support their case. This will put them to a lot of work. Make the future look bleak to them. Delay is important. It either works to your advantage or it is against you.

If you have to use a lawyer, then use a specialist in this kind of work, one who is on your side and who knows how to play a rough game. Most lawyers are rather nice people. But the one you want must be a winner. Make sure your lawyer knows how to construct a counter-claim for damages.

TACTICS AND PLAYS

Give them a warning

If they start using pressure, making strong demands and generally behaving in an impossible way, then with careful timing you can often show them that you have reached your limit. They may be trying on such tactics to test you out.

Such tactics may include mild insults to you or to your organization.

An indirect reproof, a sign that such behavior is unacceptable to you will usually be sufficient to bring them to heel. Try not to counter their attacks directly, and in the early stages try not to counter with threats of your own. Simply make it clear that this is not the way you should be treated. Your own behavior should, of course, be impeccable.

Mr. Purchase has laid out a long list of demands at the opening of the interview. The house must must be repaired, repainted, the price must come down, and so on. Replies Mr. Sells quietly: "I don't know about you, but I always find that the best deals for both parties are done between those people who get to know each other quite well first, don't you think? Would you care for a gin and tonic, or would you prefer scotch?"

It is very gentle. It is socially acceptable. But Mr. Purchase has been shown the yellow warning card.

Go down injured

When the going gets rough, it can help you to slow down the play and to bring on the trainer. Openly you show the other party that conflict is about to develop and that someone else is needed to sort out the disputed issue. So you bring in your own expert, who will "prove" your case in order to convince the other party that you are not leading them astray.

"Well, I can see you are very alarmed at our surveyor's report," says Mr. Agent, "because the signs of possible subsidence in the grounds are not obvious yet. We ourselves are concerned and we hope this will not mean that the deal will fall through. Let me bring in the surveyor who inspected the property— he will be back before the end of the week. He can tell you better than I can about it."

Find the referee

This tactic is different and is used when the two parties are locked in dispute so that they cannot obtain movement between them. Under these circumstances it can pay them to bring in an outside referee; but it should not be done unless both parties agree beforehand to abide by the referee's decisions. Even where only one party agrees, however, to abide by the decisions, the other one is still left to argue, but he is in a weaker bargaining position.

The dispute usually turns on the issue of who should be the referee. He should be a person of clear impartiality, neutral to either party and not affected by the outcome of the issue itself. He should be a person of obvious integrity and preferably unbiased by a close relationship with one party or the other.

"Well, we are not going to resolve this issue between us," says Mr. Agent. "You claim that our advertised details of the property are misleading because they show the rooms as being larger than they are, and we say that these details are only issued as a rough guide to the property. Why don't we turn it over to the Realtors' Association for their view?" "Not on your life," says Mr. Purchase. "They will only support your opinion. Let us try the State weights and measures inspector and abide by his decision." "No, we could not agree to that," replies Mr. Agent. "Suppose we took the Consumer Affairs Department's view on the matter, would that do?"

"It's like using a sledgehammer to crack a nut, but all right," says Mr. Purchase.

Look here, it is in the rules!
An established precedent is very difficult to break. It may be possible to resolve a dispute between two parties by finding out what has been done in other circumstances or in the past.

"Now that we have discovered these rather valuable Spanish coins in the garden after the exchange of contracts but before the closing, we are saying that they belong to us," says Mr. Sells, "because they are not included in our schedule of contents. You are arguing that they should belong to you because they are part of the property you are buying from us. This cannot be the first time this has happened, let us abide by what the law has said about this in the past. Do you agree?"

Kick them off the field
Be careful with disputes if you are dealing with experts. They will let you go on and on—they will stall and delay, then suddenly they will make a frightening charge at you, displaying all their strength. Their purpose is to kick you off the field.

"If you go ahead with your plan to chop down that elm tree, then I must tell you what we, as tree lovers, will do about it," says Mr. Neighbor. "We already have our plans made and these are ready for implementation the moment you say you are still going ahead with it. We shall picket your house with youngsters for an hour each morning as your neighbors go to work and again in the evening when they return. We shall invite the local press to witness it. We shall inform the local authority by telegram. We shall apply to the court for an injunction against you. We shall write to the chairman of the company where you are employed and also to your superior at work. We shall circulate a petition around the neighboring houses. We shall surround your house with bonfires on the windward side each weekend. We have carried out many such actions in the past and we have always been successful. We have never failed yet. It is, of course, entirely up to you. What do you say?"

Most people will give in. Their threats amount to illegal harassment but they will be effective in most cases.

We'll have you banned for life
Some people can turn very nasty, quite deliberately.

After the sale, Mr. Agent is trying to get his fee from Mr. Sells. "You can't have it," Mr. Sells tells him, "because we sold the house ourselves." "No," says Mr. Agent, "We did all the work, took your prospect around the house, did all the advertising."

"The buyer was a friend of mine," replies Mr. Sells. "I got him myself when you took so long to sell the property. Actually, we are going to file a claim against you because of your inefficiency. We lost money through having to get a bridging loan. We'll take you to court, see if we don't. We'll have you struck off the Realtors list. I rue the day I ever set eyes on you. Don't think we are going to pay your fee. By the time we have finished with you, you will owe us a fortune."

The counter to this is to ensure he knows your rules and to make sure you have his formal agreement to them. Tie up your terms of business tight, and make him sign before you do any work. The time to get his signature is early on, when he wants you; afterwards is too late. If you don't, you'll be caught in the "Buy now—Bargain later" trap.

Throw the game

You can always get out by paying, goes the old saying. Whatever you do, do not let disputes affect you emotionally. You might use your "shock–horror" reactions when face-to-face with the other party, but keep cool underneath.

There is no disgrace in losing. You cannot win them all. What will it cost you to go on in terms of money, and your time and energy? What are the chances of winning? If you win, what will be the net gain? If you lose, what will be the net loss? Multiply the losses and the gains by the probability factor and that will tell you whether you should simply settle and clear it all up.

You can usefully use a third party, a conduit to your opposition, to "float" the idea of a settlement, and to ask what they want. Don't commit yourself unless you can see that they are also willing to come along. If you concede too quickly, then they will try and take you for more.

If you decide to throw the game, then show them your power, make it look as if they will have a long hard fight on their hands, so they are expecting the worst. Then ask someone to convey an offer to them, making the whole thing easier.

They'll settle.

SUMMARY

Wherever conflict bargaining can break out, take special care. The potential for it exists wherever one party has a strong hold over the other, without the other party having an easy way out. It is the lack of choice and freedom which causes bargainers to use their full power when they cannot get their way by persuasion. When each party has a monopoly over the other then an unhealthy state exists.

Take care with your behavior; have patience, and game play as little as possible. Show them by example that power plays are unacceptable, do not threaten, but if you have to use your power then do so, overwhelmingly, so that you clearly frighten them. Then back off and make it easier for them. Do this very rarely; otherwise such power plays will become rooted into the structure of your relationship. Don't give in to power plays. Strength versus weakness is a bad basis for collaborative bargaining, and is the seedbed of conflict. Use coercive techniques as little as possible, turn the other cheek, have patience, behave in a trustworthy fashion, don't double-deal. If you have to break the other party then break them. But always let them come out with some relief at what they have won.

Remember also that they will have learned how to handle you the next time.

*   *   *

Now go back to the start of this chapter and complete the questionnaire again.

The Settlement | 12

Before reading the chapter, complete this learning module on closure techniques.

Q.1 *During one or several bargaining sessions, a series of closing stages are required before movement on to the next issue can be obtained. The bargainer should structure the discussion by moving from* MINOR TO MAJOR *issues.*

Q.2 *The decks should be cleared between the parties by a common agreement on the aims of the discussion and on the broad issues. At any one stage, one party usually wants something more strongly than the other party. An air of confidence will help to overcome many of the resistances as agreement is moved from.........to.........issues. Provided that the bargainer knows the other party is willing to agree, then the simplest technique is to say* "DO WE AGREE?" *and then to move on.*

Q.3 *But if there is some doubt about the intentions of the other party then a more indirect technique than "... ..." may be needed. If the other party answers "no," then the position of the bargainer is weakened. But where there is a known measure of agreement, particularly in the early stages of the movement from.........to.........issues, then this question will keep the movement going.*

Q.4 *Offering the other party an* ALTERNATIVE *choice is a good way of testing them and of securing agreement. It is the most common closing technique used by salesmen and will nearly always secure agreements on the.........issues, leaving the major sticking points until later. Asking the question "...... ...." will also help to keep the discussion flowing and the other party will get the feeling that the final overall decision is inevitable.*

Q.5 *Resisting closure techniques is easily done once they are spotted. When they provide you with.........choices, then you can back off, ask open questions, defer the decision until later.*

Q.6 *If they press their case with eagerness, constantly offering you more ....choices, then you should move away, in order to see how far they* *will make concessions to you. The time to strike is when their enthusiasm is high.*

Q.7   *The over-enthusiastic bargainer makes many little concessions towards the end, particularly after a series of gruelling sessions. He will not want to lose the deal after all the effort he has put in. Just pick up little bits of the various . . . . choices he has given you and put them together in your own package. When you have made up your mind, then you yourself can REVIEW all the difficulties which his case presents to you. Then sit quietly. He may come to you with new proposals.*

Q.8   *Both parties may need some flexibility after this . . . . of the issues, to reconstruct a more favorable package for both sides. You may need to ask for a recess to give you and them time to think.*

Q.9   *After this . . . . , if you are willing to give in to one of their demands, then you should ask them first if they are willing to concede something if you do likewise. Otherwise you will move, and they will not come with you.*

Q.10 *You could try to isolate ONE OBSTACLE that remains. Secure their agreement to the rest of the deal, provided that you can overcome this . . . . satisfactorily.*

Q.11 *If they agree on the rest of the deal, then at least you have blocked up this escape route for them. You might already have planned this . . . . earlier in the debate, knowing that you could find a solution to it in the end. You can then give them one FINAL CONCESSION to overcome it, and your deal is secured.*

Q.12 *The use of the . . . . technique shows how important it is not to give away all your case early on. Save up something which you know they want and which you know you can provide, but use it right at the end. After hours, perhaps days, of wrangling, this . . . . will be enough.*

Q.13 *But be careful that they do not use your own enthusiasm for clinching the deal against you. Right at the end, just before the paper is signed, they could make one unexpected demand, thereby forcing you into making this . . . . unexpectedly. You can resist this fairly easily, but only if you are expecting the move.*

The Settlement | 12

When Tony Jacobs left his customer's office he knew he had secured the deal. The customer knew it also. Both were wrong.

For several weeks, the customer had been searching various suppliers of overhead projectors for use in training courses. He wanted six machines, portable, and at the lower price end of the market, at around $275 each. One supplier in New Jersey appeared to offer the best machine.

Tony Jacobs had known the customer socially for many years. The customer telephoned him to ask if Tony Jacobs's company, a local supplier of audio-visual equipment, could match the New Jersey deal. Tony went to see him immediately; his offer was just a little higher in price and his machine was just a little heavier in weight but these appeared to be marginal factors for the customer. Their old amiable friendship was renewed, and Tony Jacobs left the meeting in fair spirits. His mistake was to cost him not only the immediate $550 worth of business but also a more substantial repeat order.

Failure in bargaining is not so much due to the things which we do which are wrong; failure is due more to not doing something which is crucial. The bargaining sins are the sins of omission, not the sins of commission.

Hint for bargainers:

> *Our ruin is caused not so much by what we say*
> *as by what we do not say.*

The world abounds with examples of people who do not ask for what they want. Buyers do not ask for discounts. Salesmen do not ask for orders. Financial managers do not ask for their bills to be paid. Chief executives do not ask their staff for greater efforts. Staff people do not ask their bosses for salary increases.

To be sure, most people do these things some of the time. The previous paragraph may even seem incomprehensible to you—your own world may be inhabited by people who do all of these things most of the time. But some people are very bad at asking for what they want. (Out of all the salary increases you can remember over the years, how many have been *given* to you and what proportion have you asked for?) And for the rest of us, shrewd bargainers that we may be in our business lives, we still experience occasions when it would have paid us to have asked the price first, before we bought something.

Tony Jacobs' expensive mistake was to forget to ask for the order there and then, when he met the customer. The interest and enthusiasm were high, then;

the customer would have been pleased to give him a commitment to buy subject to having one look at a demonstration machine. The customer would have driven home, happy that the decision was made. But Tony left the matter on trust. He arranged for the customer to see the machine next morning. Instead,

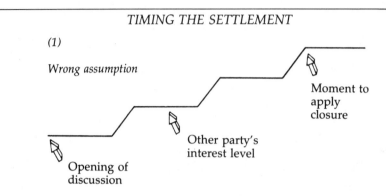

TIMING THE SETTLEMENT

(1)

Wrong assumption

Moment to apply closure

Other party's interest level

Opening of discussion

When a bargainer wants to close he must get the timing right. The other party must be "ready" emotionally. His interest should be high at the time. There should be an emotional bond between the parties. The other party's interest does not rise in a series of steps throughout the discussion as each new facet of the presentation is revealed.

What happens is that his interest moves up and down in a series of waves. He may be interested at one moment, but if the chance to close is lost then he may immediately become bored and raise new resistances. The moment to close can occur at almost any time. It's seldom too early to try but it can often be too late.

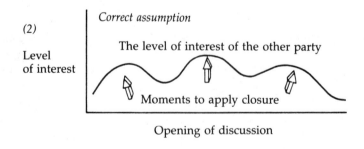

Correct assumption

(2)

Level of interest

The level of interest of the other party

Moments to apply closure

Opening of discussion

the customer drove home thinking. He thought, why pay more than I need to; and why buy heavier machines when they will have to be carried around? He felt a trifle silly to be making a deal on the basis of his friendship with his old chum, after all his careful and logical search of possible suppliers. He knew he was not committed to Tony. So the next morning he made an excuse to avoid the demonstration, and he bought the New Jersey machines.

That is an example of what a salesman would call a failure to close the business. It happens in bargaining, also, but closure needs special care. Two parties are involved, each wanting something from the other. Each party faces varying degrees of winning or losing, and the settlement confirms the position. In Tony Jacobs's case, he definitely "lost," but the customer did not necessarily win— this would depend upon the deal he finally made, and would relate to his expectations for that deal.

All the bargaining skills in the world will not help if you do not close the deal properly. In practice several stages of the deal may need to be "closed" and agreed before the discussion can move on. A sense of timing is needed by both the parties involved. The discussion may be quick, it may be long—before you start you cannot always tell.

But sometimes you will need to have an edge, a technique, just to nudge the other party past his state of reluctance or inertia and into a commitment. Such closure techniques should be used with care. The overuse of pressure tactics will cause some parties to withdraw. They simply must not notice what you are doing, the closing techniques must seem to be a natural part of the discussion. Closing techniques are necessary because at any one time, one party usually wants the deal more than the other, although they may not show it. They must bring the reluctant party with them therefore.

The most common tactic for securing the decision is to offer the other party the choice between two alternatives. "Would you rather that we do this, or would you prefer that we do that, instead?" It seems natural, but it is a pressure tactic, because the way in which the question is posed does not allow room for the other party to say that he prefers neither alternative, or no deal at all. It is gentle, however, because if the other party demurs at either choice then the bargainer can still carry on with the discussion. If the bargainer asks for the decision instead by saying, "Do you agree on this, then?" he is in some difficulty if the other party says "No." Be careful, however. Studies show that this is the most favored principal closing technique and is used by 70% of salesmen all the time. Professional buyers laugh, every time they hear it. They know exactly what the man is up to.

Throughout the closing stages, a posture of quiet confidence should be adopted. The other party will need reassurance, perhaps, that they are making the right decision. A confident manner combined with an implicit acceptance that the deal will be done will usually see the bargainer through the odd moments of uncertainty.

You can find out if they are ready for the decision sometimes by testing them a little. If you move the discussion on to the question of timing, or to the question of delivery, or terms of business or credit, then if the other party is contemplating a favorable decision they will discuss these matters with interest. They are not usually central to the decision, but if they are being considered with interest then you can take it that the other party has made up its mind.

In an earlier chapter we mentioned the example of a company making a wine filter kit to supply to home winemakers. The executive concerned with this project felt he was paying too much for the basic plastic component, which was produced by one supplier who held the tools for doing the job. The tools, being expensive, were the property of the customer.

The executive searched for alternative quotations. He had a strong reason for trying to force down the cost of the product. The supplier heard that quotations were being sought from competitors and asked what was going on. The executive took two colleagues to see the supplier, and laid before them the competitive facts. The executive was absolutely convinced that he was going to reduce the price. The supplier refused absolutely to consider it. Whatever the pressure put on by the executive, he resisted it absolutely. Not a single concession was made apart from a small one right at the end. He stuck hard on the quality of his product and the quality of his service.

Now the executive was in a quandary. He did not know whether he could swing his own company behind any move to take the business away from the supplier. The supplier was too well-known to company personnel. Only the executive himself really wanted to increase the profitability of the product. No one else cared much. The executive asked for a recess as the argument began to be heated. This was his favorite device for giving the other party time to think. He hoped that the weaker members of the supplier's bargaining team would put pressure on the leader to give way. He let them cool off, and realize that the business was at stake for them. Upon returning to the meeting, the executive and his colleagues had modified their stance but they found to their horror that the supplier had not moved his at all.

The executive's team collapsed. By taking an extreme stand, and by risking the whole business, the supplier continued to make the product and supplies it still to this day. He had been counseled to take such a stand secretly by one of the staff in the executive's company, who did not like his own team leader.

Now in this case, settlement meant winning for one party and losing for the other. This is fraught with hazard, for open conflict can break out at the final stages. Such conflict can often concentrate upon relatively small issues, issues which at one time earlier in the discussion would have been traded away easily. Such small issues are often major snags at the final stage.

Throughout the bargaining process both parties usually search for collaboration. They trade concessions. In doing so, each gives up a little of his own power and steadily becomes more committed to doing the deal with the other party. It becomes clear that a deal is "on." At this point there is a danger of conflict breaking out if one party becomes too extreme in its demands.

Once the settlement area can be defined, the skilled bargainer will take stock and review the situation. He will attempt to define the outstanding issues clearly. He may make a comparison of the remaining arguments, on both sides. Before going for agreement he must be certain that he has obtained all the concessions he can and he must develop a strategy for obtaining the remaining ones. It is only too easy to obtain what we want from the principal deal, to find that we have conceded as much or more than we have gained from the marginal issues. Provided that he brings the other party with him through these stages then all will be well. A deadline for the final agreement can be set and few problems will remain.

Obstacles to the closure

However, you may find that while you may be eager to secure the deal, the other party is not yet convinced and is not ready to come with you. This is a dangerous situation. If you try to "close" the deal, then the other party may sense your eagerness and hold off. You will be making a one-way journey all by yourself. You will make the final concessions and he will make none. You may be unable to secure the business at all.

Sensitivity and timing are the keynotes. Eagerness is disaster. One of the world's largest paint companies was contracting for a major promotion. It had been negotiated between the sales director for the paint company and the sales promotion company's president. The promotion was designed to assist sales of the products through distributors. The sales promotion company had proposed taking a commission on all the painting and purchases connected with the proposal, plus a service fee for handling the scheme. Telephoning the client's sales director to find out if he had secured the contract, the sales promotion company's president was told that his fee was too high, and that the client's financial director would be in touch with him. At the same time he was asked if the scheme could be mounted to start on a specified date.

At that moment, the president of the sales promotion company knew he had secured the business. All he had to do was to play a game on pricing. When the financial director telephoned him he was out of the office, and he did not telephone back. The financial director telephoned again and again: he was out of the office and did not telephone back. He was using delay to press home his advantage. In the end, the client sales director came through to his office to confirm that the scheme was being planned to start on the specified day.

All the president had to do then was to telephone the client's financial director, full of apologies, resist all attempts at cutting the fee, but making one small concession on one aspect of the expenses. He got the deal at his price. The customer had been too keen to show that he was going to buy.

When the other party refuses to argue the settlement with you, there may be a number of reasons. First, he may be avoiding the decision, perhaps in the hope that something better will turn up, or perhaps in the hope that delay will weaken you and you will make a better offer.

He may be fearful of the risk involved. He may be uncertain of the alternatives available to him, he may be unable to be certain that his own colleagues will agree with his decision. What might go wrong later? If he commits to the deal, will everyone be happy? Is he making a mistake in not leaving things as they are?

Some decisions have to be pressed home, however, otherwise people will never make them. Few people ever volunteer themselves for life insurance policies; they have to be sold. Few people volunteer for double glazing, that has to be sold. Few people ask to see salesmen from *Encyclopaedia Britannica*; they have to be dug out as sales prospects and then be sold the volumes. Few people become Jehovah's Witnesses without being tackled about it first by a follower.

In all these cases, the prospects for these goods and services must be enthusiastically "sold" and taken through to the close. Yet, at the close, too much eagerness is self-defeating. They need careful hand-holding. They need reassurance, above all else. It takes a confident manner and style to lead to the closing stages. Setting deadlines for the remaining issues can help, because the movement which is then obtained provides a reassuring effect in itself. The interest remains high.

Signalling the final offer

There comes a moment when you want to make it absolutely clear that you have reached your final offer. This time you are not playing, there is no bluffing involved. When you reach this stage you must know what to do, and you must also be able to recognize by the words and actions of the other party when he is also signalling his final offer.

Incidentally, this "final" offer may also be the first offer. Where a quick kill is required, then the final offer is signalled immediately and a deadline is set for the decision. The other party knows therefore that the first offer is the last.

The final offer signals can be observed in the behavior of the bargainer when married up to the actual words he uses. When you want them to know that you have come to the end of the argument, that you are prepared for breakdown, that no more concessions are possible, this is what you should do.

You should leave yourself absolutely no way out from your position. You should employ a minimum of argument. Use short sentences. Make certain that you give yourself no alternative. Give brief answers to their questions. You should sit up, your arms can be folded, you act as though you are ready for separation. Your papers should be squared away. And, most important of all, you should use a tone of finality.

In a major London hotel, a conference was being staged for a large party due to start at 10:00 a.m. The organizer arrived at 8:00 a.m. to find that two major conferences were booked at the hotel at the same time and that his conference had been booked into the worst room of the two available.

He brought the banqueting manager to see him in the reception area. (He did not go to see the banqueting manager.) He told the manager loudly and firmly, in front of the hotel guests, that the situation was not acceptable. He told him that he wanted the better room, that there would be no argument about it, and that he would expect arrangements to have been completed by 9:30. Then he walked out of the hotel.

The manager was in a quandary. The customer meant it clearly. There would be a dreadful row if he did not change the rooms over. Conference visitors would start ariving soon. If he were to change the rooms over, he had to move fast, before the rival conference organizer arrived.

He switched the rooms. He had no option. By stating his demand and then walking away, the first conference organizer had secured the decision.

Tip for conference organizers:

Turn up early.

You could signal your final offer another way. You might try passing an informal message to the other party, outside the meeting, to the effect that you are about to make your final offer. You can only do this once after long and complex sessions have exhausted all possibilities. By doing this, and by providing one final concession which you have held in reserve all this time for just such a contingency as this, you will secure the deal.

Final offer strategies

When two parties come close together, when the dancing is over, the most exciting time arrives. This is the time when the barriers are down, both parties are telling each other what they want, the risk of collision is strong and the emotions run high. Luckily, both parties want a successful conclusion at this stage. It pays to keep a light manner at this moment. Don't get heavy. Smile, laugh, but keep a cool head. If the other party gets angry, lighten the tone. Keep the discussion open and flowing. But be on your guard—the penalties for losing at this stage can be quite high. In a second, one unthought-out concession can ruin all the careful planning and preparation which have gone into the process so far.

People often make use of precedence and past practice to guide them through the dangers of final offers. "We have settled it this way before, why do we not do so again?" they might say. The logic of this approach is its strength and it may be difficult to resist unless a better formula can be put forward.

A different but very common formula is to "split the difference." But be careful, the difference need not necessarily be split down the middle. It can be two-thirds to us and one-third to them. If you suggest this formula then be certain that you *secure their agreement* in advance to the idea of coming some way towards you. You might say, "To solve the problem, will you be prepared to move some way towards me, if I move some way towards you?" If you do not do this, then they will play an end game against you.

They will let you make your offer of a 50/50 split and they will confirm your new position. They themselves have not made any commitment to move at all, and they can then stand pat on their previous offer. It is difficult for you then to retreat to your old position because they now know you are willing to move. By holding on, they can get you to move further.

Generally, the first bargainer to name his final figure is the one who loses. This is because the other party can go to the other extreme. Splitting the difference then moves the settlement nearer the other party's expected result.

You can use phrases such as "Take it or leave it" or "This is my last and final offer" and this stops you from going any further. You must get the timing right. And you must know that at the moment you make this closing statement, they want the deal. Otherwise they will withdraw and you cannot go after them without losing your credibility.

Never let the other party see that your resistance is only an act of personal will on your part. They will take this as a personal insult and will counter your will with theirs, or they will get angry.

Always allow them to see why you cannot go any further. "This is all I've got," is a marvelous phrase for a final closure statement. But "I am not prepared to pay a penny more" is a poor statement and will draw a counterattack.

Crowding, and end games

After the settlement is completed, be on your guard. It might start all over again with an end game. This game is designed to work on the pleasure and excitement of the other party when it is at its highest, when he thinks he has secured the deal. Then he discovers to his chagrin that the other party has not yet fully committed in every respect but is prepared to, provided that one little final concession is made.

A protracted hassle between a boat builder and his customer ended up with the builder getting rid of a problem boat, but at a very low price. He was contracted by the customer to do some work on the boat before delivery. The customer was telephoned, one week before delivery, and was told that some extra little damage had been spotted on the boat and that this had been missed in the surveyor's report. It would add $500 to the price. What did he, the customer, want the boat builder to do about it? The customer paid up.

Was it true, or was it a bluff? Was it an end game? Only the boat builder knows. But the tactic could have been handled better by the customer if he had expected the game to be played. He could have backed off from the deal. He could have told the builder to talk with the surveyor. He could have offered to split the extra cost with the builder, the owner, and himself. He did none of these things. Why? Simply because he was looking forward to taking delivery of the boat the following weekend and $500 was not going to stand in his way.

Crowding is a different stratagem. What you do is to call a taxi, find you have to fly to the next meeting, find an urgent excuse to leave. If you get the timing right, particularly when they are momentarily in a position of weakness, then you will find that they will agree to your final little demand to secure the deal. But they must not suspect what you are doing.

A contract was being secured for the employment of a large number of temporary staff for a big project. The agency concerned had to recruit the staff from overseas. The agency's proposition was to be agreed to after the agency executive had been shown around the factory. The agency executive knew that the client wanted to try to reduce the charges in the proposal. So he led the way slowly through the discussion on the proposal without getting to the section on costing. It was implied that this would be discussed later in the day. The agency executive was shown around the factory, he stayed a long time there, and then discovered to his dismay that he was close to being late for his flight home. The client was concerned, rushed him to the airport. The client completely forgot that he meant to discuss the costs and to obtain a rebate, until he saw the agency man's plane flying into the distance. By then, of course, it was too late. He did not know it, but he had been crowded.

Recording the deal

Whoever keeps the minutes of the meeting has a controlling hand on the decisions.

Hint for bargainers:

> *Always save them the work of keeping the*
> *minutes of the meetings. You do it.*
> *It will make you a fortune.*

After each meeting it is important to write up a short report and publish it to the other party as well as to your own side. This ensures that agreements cannot be rescinded later. Such a document has almost the power of law, in that it is so useful should there be a dispute later.

The document can also be used to help persuade the other side. The other party usually has other people behind him whom he must influence. If the minutes of each meeting record your agreed upon analysis of his problem; your agreed upon solution to his problem; and the benefits to him of your proposition, then he will use this as an aid when he comes to talk to his own people about the deal.

In a long and complex deal, stretching over several sessions, it may be necessary to read over the agreed upon minutes as each point is settled. The notes can then be presented for agreement by the other side and little final confusion will exist. This is particularly important in conflict bargaining situations when there is little trust existing on either side.

If the other party presents you with their minutes of the meeting, then watch out. They are doing to you what you should be doing to them—don't take the lazy way out. Make your own notes and compare your notes with their report. Reject their minutes whenever the angle is shaped in their direction. Remember that minutes nearly have the power of law if they have been circulated and errors have not been rejected.

When a large marina was built in a south coast town, there was a storm of local opposition to the plans. The developers asked local sailing and seaports interests to support their application for planning permission at public meetings and so on. The boat builder mentioned previously was one of those who promised his support in exchange for an agreement that he could have the rights to the boat repairing work in the marina. The local sailing club also provided vigorous support in exchange for the understanding that full clubhouse facilities and dinghy facilities would be provided when the marina was completed, and all at a fair charge.

Being professionals at the development game, the marina company took care not to specify these commitments in writing. Being amateurs at the game, the boat builder, the sailing club, and others, were all happy with the oral commitments of the marina developers.

Let me ask you. After reading this book, do you believe that the boat builder now enjoys a thriving repair business in the heart of the marina? Does the local sailing club now have any facility in the marina, or are they excluded to make way for big, expensive boats?

They could have been there today, if they had used their power when they had it (before planning permission was granted) and if they had secured written commitments from the developers.

In other words, they should have closed the deals properly.

CLOSURE TACTICS AND PLAYS

Scoring the goal direct from the kick off
This is a nice tactic because it saves a great deal of time and expense. Its success depends upon having a high reputation to start with, knowing enough about the competition to be able to knock them out quickly, and having a good excuse ready as to why the offer cannot be repeated, so that a deadline can be set. The demand must be strong and the offer must be good, however.

"Look," says Mr. Sells, "I'll be frank with you. You have seen that the house is good value for the $200,000 we are asking for it. But I have just learned that my firm is sending me to an overseas branch, so I must decide quickly whether to sell it now or to keep it and to ask the agent to rent it for me. I have got to leave in a month. I will drop the price by $25,000 but you would have to undertake to complete the deal within four weeks."

Shall we call it a draw?
Be very careful with this tactic. In skillful hands it can be a devastating play. Its success depends upon the loser failing to quantify the value of each party's concessions. One party reviews the *number* of concessions made by each party, and surprisingly finds out that his side has made more concessions than the other. He then announces a draw. The tactic can only be played when both parties are approaching exhaustion. If this tactic does not work, because the other party begins to add up the value of the concessions, then there is a more advanced play which involves granting one last concession. This later game is called: "You won after all."

Says Mr. Sells, "I have made a list of all the fifteen things you wanted us to do before you buy the house. In return you have agreed to five things we wanted. It sounds more than equal to me. Shall we leave it there?"

The following are all end games, designed to catch the other party unawares. For their success they depend upon surprise; each can be countered easily if it is anticipated. They are usually applied when both parties are nearing exhaustion, and the loser is in a state of temporary weakness and indecision. The extra pressure is enough to tip the balance.

The game's over, now
The tactic is to assume that the previous discussion was the final one and nothing remains to be said. This blocks the loser from asking for anything else.

"My dear fellow," says Mr. Purchase, "It's much too late to start talking about a price for the lighting fixtures and fittings. I have got my lawyer briefed now, we are fully committed on the basis of the deal we agreed. No, no, the lighting fixtures and fittings form part of the house we saw and they are part of the purchase price we have paid. Sorry, but you made a deal."

It's either a goal, or we won't play
This involves a straightforward threat to pull out of the deal altogether unless a demand is agreed to. Its success depends upon the other party wanting to do the deal badly, and believing that the deal is probably going through. The loser has been lulled throughout into a sense of false security.

"I am most awfully sorry, I don't quite know how to tell you this," said Mr. Sells. "Our own house purchase has fallen through and it looks as though we will have to take this one off the market. It is a terrible disappointment to you, I know. The trouble is that my bank wants me to find another $5,000 for the deposit, and we are stretched to our limit. Don't know what to suggest to you."

Implicit in this is the idea that the other guy coughs up the missing $5,000.

The whistle is due any minute
This is a straightforward deadline imposed for the deal.

"Could you let me know by next Wednesday whether you want to go ahead?" says Mr. Sells. "I must let these other people know by then if they can look over the house."

Scoring in overtime
This tactic demands that a final concession is kept in reserve all the way through the discussion. It must be something that the other party wants, but which has been deliberately fought over early on and the demand was refused. Then, to clinch the deal, the concession is made.

"We have enjoyed talking with you and we would like to think of your living here, but we seem to be getting bogged down," says Mr. Sells. "I tell you what. We said earlier that we could not include the carpets in the deal. If you do the deal now, then we will leave the stair carpets and the two smaller bedroom carpets. It will cost us about $1,500 extra ourselves and save you that amount. We wouldn't offer it to anyone else! What do you say?"

SUMMARY

Closing is largely the art of timing. It is common to find that a bargaining session can apparently take an endless amount of time without much movement taking place. And then for some reason great issues become resolved quite speedily, concessions are exchanged, and the final details are sewn up in a matter of minutes. Settling the deal requires both parties to be in an emotional state which is ready for it. But one party makes the significant move which starts it.

This emotional state may exist several times during the course of conversation. The common means of seeing if the other party is ready to do the deal is to test him out. Ask some probing question which relates to circumstances which will arise after the deal is completed. If he continues with this conversation then he is thinking of completing. Secure agreement on minor issues. Summarize where you both stand. Then on the major issues give him a couple of choices—would he prefer to do the deal this way or that way? Give him plenty of reassurance; express confidence yourself but do not be too eager for the close otherwise he may spot it and squeeze more concessions from you.

When you make your final offer make every gesture possible to indicate that you have come to the end. Do not help the conversation along. They will realize that there is no more to come from you.

Answers to Questions |

CHAPTER 2

Q.1   *(a)* −5
(b) +5
(c) +10   You must "case" the prospect first. The drivers know the background.
(d) −10
(e) 0

Q.2   *(a)* +5   Don't give up bargaining power.
(b) 0
(c) −5
(d) +10   Make them come to you, first.

Q.3   *(a)* 0   Not on a personal issue like this.
(b) −5   You have shown your intentions too early.
(c) +5
(d) +10   Strengthen your power a little first.

Q.4   *(a)* −10   They'll select what they want and nail you down.
(b) −5
(c) +5
(d) 0
(e) +10

Q.5   *(a)* 0
(b) +10   You work in a team.
(c). −5
(d) −10

Q.6   *(a)* −10   You will lose contact with them and infuriate them. You are challenging them to do their worst.
(b) +3   A bit too close to your aim for comfort.
(c) +5

> (*d*) 0   The productivity offer can come later and be traded in the deal.

Q.7   (*a*) +10   He might offer more than $180.
    (*b*) −5   Though you might score more if the police are hard on your tail.
    (*c*) 0   Not bad, but you are signaling that $180 is not your final price.
    (*d*) +5

Scores

Above 36	Very good. Life has taught you well.
11–35	Fair result. The book will help.
Below 10	Don't give up—you have only just started the book.

CHAPTER 3

The highest quality answers score at one end or the other of the scale. The test is based upon an achievement motivation test; improving results and a drive towards higher skills can be expected from those with a higher score. There is an element of achievement motivation which is independent of work or family background and also independent of the level of present skill.

To calculate your score, give each correct answer the value of 5. The other end of the scale will carry a value therefore of 1. A or E = 5 or 1. B or D = 4 or 2; C = 3.

Question	Best answer	Points for your answer
1	A	...
2	E	...
3	A	...
4	E	...
5	E	...
6	A	...
7	E	...
8	E	...
9	E	...
10	E	...
11	A	...
12	A	...
13	E	...
14	A	...

Scores

Below 42	Very low achievement motivation.
42–50	Get into easier situations where you can be more successful. Success is a strong encouragement.
51–59	This might take you out of the absolutely top class: but you could make it.
60 and above	Very high achievement motivation.

CHAPTER 4

Q.1 You should really approach all of them to see what they can each do for you. It is a lot of money, and effort spent now in terms of research would pay off handsomely in the future. Otherwise, the personal financial analyst would give you the best all-around advice.

(*a*) (*b*) (*c*) 0 points; (*d*) (*f*) (*g*) 3 points; (*e*) 5 points; (*h*) 7 points.

Q.2 If we seek information from others, they can only provide it within the framework of their own experience and knowledge. Each person will be biased in the direction of his experience; and some of them may have a personal interest in guiding your decisions in their direction. A stockbroker cannot help but guide you towards stocks and shares; an insurance broker towards pension policies and so on. Even a bank manager may have an interest in guiding your decision towards investments in his own subsidiaries.

(*a*) Stockbroker — **1** = 5 points / **7** = 1 point

(*b*) Unit-linked insurance agent (He will recommend his own company) — **5** = 5 points

(*c*) Insurance broker — **6** = 5 points / **5** = 4 points / **4** = 5 points

(But he will recommend companies which pay brokers' commission; not all companies do so)

(*d*) Bank manager — **7** = 5 points / **2** = 4 points / **3** = 3 points

(*e*) Personal financial analyst — **1** = 5 points / **4** = 5 points / **3** = 4 points

(He understands about the problems of
tax planning)

(f)   Lawyer   **7** = 5 points
                                                     4 = 4 points
                                                     2 = 4 points

(He leans towards safety and protection)

(g)   Accountant   **4** = 5 points
                                                     6 = 4 points
                                                     3 = 3 points
                                                     8 = 3 points

(He thinks of tax advantages)

You should normally score high on this test. It is not difficult, although it needs
a little understanding of investment. 30 or more is good. Above 20 is adequate.

CHAPTER 5

Q.1   *(a)* − 10   *(b)* + 5   *(c)* + 5   *(d)* + 10

Q.2   These score + 1: a, e, g, l, m, p, s
           These score − 1: c, d, i, j, n, r, t

Q.3   *(a)* + 5   *(b)* − 5   *(c)* − 10
           From a position of weakness you must find out how the land lies before
           you can ask him for anything.

Q.4   *(a)* + 10   *(b)* 0   *(c)* − 5
           The reverse rule applies to the above. Get the facts first in writing before
           you can be committed by a face-to-face meeting.

Q.5   *(a)* − 10
           (b) + 10   Good for your status.
           (c) 0
           (d) − 5

Q.6   *(a)* + 10   If you don't get it now, you won't get it at all; don't
                           let your status get in the way of the money. Grab it
                           and go.
           (b) − 10
           (c) − 10
           (d) − 1,000

Q.7 (*a*) + 5 (*b*)0 (*c*) − 10 (*d*) + 10

Scores

55 or more	Good—you are on target.
35–54	I wonder if you could be more of a salesman than a buyer. Bite a little harder.
20–34	You are a nice person—people like you, you are warm, open.
Less than 20	Start the book again.

CHAPTER 6

Q.1 (*a*) + 5   (*b*) + 4   (*c*) + 1   (*d*) 0   (*e*) − 3   (*f*) − 5

Q.2 —   —   (*c*) + 3   (*d*) + 7   (*e*) 0   (*f*) − 10

Q.3 (*a*) 0   (*b*) + 5   (*c*) + 4   (*d*) + 2   (*e*) − 1   (*f*) − 5

Q.4 The correct answer is the same as you gave for question 1, i.e., your best possible deal. This answer will score + 5 for you. All other answers score 0.

Q.5 (*a*) − 5   (*b*) 0   (*c*) − 2   (*d*) + 5

When you see him you want to have the full facts available about competitive offers.

Q.6 (a) 0   (b) 0   (c) + 5

Q.7 (a) − 5   (b) + 7   (c) 0   (d) + 5

You are being moved too far away from your original objective. You have other options available to you. Is he the only dealer in the world? Why not wait until the end of the season? You could telephone around to find out which dealer is holding high inventory levels.

Q.8 —Ask him for the Mercury at $1,340 or thereabouts because he will increase his sales: SCORES 5*

---

*An offer of $1,380 or thereabouts is worth 4 points. Asking for his best price is worth 3 points, provided that he has been shown the alternative quotations first.

—Tell him reasons why you have no more money available than, say, $1,000 net, after selling your engine: SCORES 5

—Ask him to sell your existing Mercury for you acting as agent:
          SCORES 5

—Explain that you are really going to buy a Yamaha from his competitor, but if he can match the best deal you will stay with him:
          SCORES 5

—Explain that servicing will be worth about $300 a year at least to him, which totals nearly $1,500, until you trade in the engine for another one in 5 years time: SCORES 10

—He can clear his old inventory: SCORES 3

—He can turn his inventory into cash: SCORES 3

Q.9   *(a)* − 5   *(b)* 0   *(c)* + 5   *(d)* + 3

Don't give in too quickly.

Q.10   *(a)* − 5   *(b)* + 5   *(c)* 0

Q.11   *(a)* + 8   *(b)* + 7   *(c)* + 3   *(d)* − 10

Scores

65   You are doing all right, but be careful you do not overdo the demanding bit. He must win, too.

40–64   Keep going, perhaps leave yourself a little more room, and do not be afraid to bid high.

0–39   You are probably making the mistake of rushing things. Deals take time; you are going in with offers you know they will accept first off.

A minus score: Are you sure you are reading the right book?

CHAPTER 7 LEARNING MODULE

Q.1   Open
Q.2   Open
Q.3   Open
          Open
Q.4   Open
Q.5   Leading
Q.6   Open
          Leading
Q.7   Open

	Leading
Q.8	Leading
Q.9	Confirmation
Q.10	Confirmation
Q.11	Confirmation
Q.12	Confirmation
	Leading
Q.13	Weakening
Q.14	Weakening
Q.15	Weakening
Q.16	Weakening
Q.17	Supportive
Q.18	Supportive
	Weakening
Q.19	Weakening
	Supportive
Q.20	Supportive
Q.21	Benefits
Q.22	Benefits
Q.23	Proof
	Benefit
Q.24	Benefits
	Benefits
	Benefit
	Proof
Q.25	Benefits

CHAPTER 8

Q.2	Re-directed question
Q.3	Re-directed question
Q.4	Re-directed question
Q.5	Re-directed question
Q.6	Showing agreement
Q.7	Showing agreement
Q.8	Re-directed question: showing agreement
Q.9	Showing agreement
Q.10	Reason to agree
Q.11	Reason to agree
Q.12	Reason to agree
Q.13	Comparison: third party reference: offer a trial
Q.14	Comparison: third party reference: offer a trial
Q.15	Rebut

Q.16   Rebut
Q.17   Rebut
Q.18   Rebut
Q.19   "It is up to you"
Q.20   "It is up to you"

CHAPTER 9

Q.1   *(a)* 0   *(b)* + 5   *(c)* − 5   *(d)* − 10
Get them to commit themselves first. Then you are free to move to the other extreme.

Q.2   *(a)* + 5   *(b)* + 5   *(c)* + 10   *(d)* − 10

Q.3   *(a)* − 5   weaken   *(b)* + 10   *(c)* + 5   *(d)* − 10
                       them
(Don't be silly. How are you going to feed your wife and family if you give advice like this? Wait until later.)

Q.4   *(a)* − 10   *(b)* 0   *(c)* − 5   *(d)* + 5   *(e)* + 10

Q.5   *(a)* 0   *(b)* − 5   *(c)* + 8   (if he doesn't come now, you can
still come back for him); (d) + 5. Technically correct, but you expect him to work this out in the middle of a Force 10 storm? What are you, an optimist or something?

Q.6   *(a)* 0   *(b)* + 5   *(c)* − 5   *(d)* − 10

Q.7   There is no need to score this. Everyone gets it right.

Q.8   *(a)* 0   *(b)* + 5   *(c)* − 10   *(d)* − 5   *(e)* − 5

Scores

30 or more	Good. You treat pricing questions seriously, you get into the right kind of posture for closing and you are not in any way naïve.
20–29	Fair, but your problem is that you think price is just another part of the presentation. It is not. It requires a highly specialized approach all of its own. It is the way you present price, as much as price itself, which gets you the result.
10–19	You are being skinned, and you might not always realize it.

9 or less   I like you, I really do. And so does the rest of the world. Lend me $10, would you? If you have it left, that is.

CHAPTER 10

Q.1   *(a)* − 10   *(b)* 0   *(c)* − 10   *(d)* + 5

Q.2   *(a)* + 10   *(b)* + 5   *(c)* 0   *(d)* − 5
It does matter.

Q.3   *(a)* 0   *(b)* + 10   *(c)* + 5   *(d)* − 5
He will expect a bargain.

Q.4   *(a)* − 10   Start reading the book at the beginning again.
          (b) − 5   Too strong at this stage. They have heard it all before.
          (c) + 5   You need more information about what alternatives are available both to him and to you.
          (d) 0   His telephone at home is busy on Sundays. He has been around a bit, too.

Q.5   *(a)* − 5   You have got more power than this. How else are they going to fill the vacant rooms, if they turn you away?
          (b) 0   Too early. How do you know you can trust them?
          (c) + 10   Hold out for it, for the time being. You will have to concede in the end but make them do a little work for it, as well as make some concessions on their side.
          (d) + 5   They may find it difficult to hold third parties to an agreement with *your* travel agent. You may be asking for the impossible. But it is worth a try.

Q.6   *(a)* 0   *(b)* − 5   *(c)* + 5   *(d)* + 10

Scores
35–50   Yes, you stand firm when the going gets rough.
20–35   Take more time to think. Plan more carefully.
          You may be leaving it all to your instinct.
19 or less   If you want something badly enough then you must find a way to push for it. It does not mean using aggression, that is not your way. But it does mean using persistence and not giving in too easily.

CHAPTER 11

Q.1   *(a)* + 5
          (b) − 10   If you do this kind of thing, that is probably why you are heading for the rocks.

(c) + 10
(d) − 5

Q.2   *(a)* − 5   You really are too nice.
          (b) + 5
          (c) − 10   Try for a job in sales.
          (d) + 10   It's normal. You will not create conflict. They want
                           your business. But modify it with close warm sup-
                           pliers.

Q.3   *(a)* − 10   They'll know about it all right; probably when they
                           don't receive it. They will not trust you again.
          (b) + 10   Nothing else for it.
          (c) 0   He might be right; it could damage other deals.
          (d) − 5   It's your deal, not his.

Q.4   *(a)* − 5   *(b)* − 10   *(c)* + 10   *(d)* + 5
          There is no harm in stalling. Let them propose the productivity deal.

Q.5   *(a)* 0
          (b) − 10   You must get the emotion down first. If you try these,
                           she'll scream and you will have 100 spectators in a
                           minute.
          (c) − 10
          (d) − 5
          (e) + 10   It is the only way. You should have gone to the arrivals
                           lounge in disguise.

Q.6   *(a)* 0
          (b) − 10   If you use this heavy leverage, you will create conflict.
                           He may agree at that moment, because he has no
                           option. But he will seek revenge.
          (c) + 5
          (d) + 10   Professional.

Q.7   *(a)* + 10
          (b) − 7   You have no bargaining power afterwards. You have
                           done the work, but they will hold the money.
          (c) 0
          (d) + 5   They play a rough game in the film industry and they
                           are quite used to this. But you'll get nothing at all, if
                           they *can* find someone else. And you will not get work
                           in the future.

Q.8   *(a)* + 10   This is the rational answer; but it is too cold a reaction.

(b) – 10   Does not make logical sense, but it is emotionally appealing.

(c) – 5

(d) + 5

(e) 0   Got to give you marks for bravery; you will lose, but you will learn, too. (You are not being fair on your other suppliers. You will drag them down with you, and it is not their fault.)

Q.9   (a) – 10   You will be a hostage to fortune and they will all fight you.

(b) + 5   You will have to learn first; and to build upon success.

(c) – 5   Half the problem is with management probably. The workforce will skin you, unless they are genuinely willing to go along.

(d) 0   You have got to lead them; they might not trust you. Morale might get worse.

(e) – 5   It is very tempting; but you will not easily graft on new managers.

(f) + 10   They don't have to like you, but they do have to trust you. You must be a man of your word.

Scores

Several answers are possible here, for each case is distinct. It is very difficult to obtain very high scores on this subject.

55–90   You have been here before. This is the meat and stuff of your life. Just remember that collaborative bargaining is different and requires a gentler approach. Don't use strong-arm tactics in everyday life. People don't like it; and the tactics do not always work.

30–54   A normal score.

Up to 29   Conflict bargaining is not everyone's game. Remember that bargaining needs a little coercion sometimes.

CHAPTER 12

Q.2   Minor to major

Q.3   Do we agree?

Minor to major

Q.4   Minor

Do we agree?

Q.5   Alternative

Q.6   Alternative

Q.7   Alternative

Q.8   Review
Q.9   Review
Q.10   One obstacle
Q.11   One obstacle
Q.12   One obstacle
          Final concession
Q.13   Final concession

Index